Letters to Marc about Jesus

Letters to Marc about Jesus

Henri J. M. Nouwen

Translated by
Hubert Hoskins

Darton, Longman and Todd
London

First published in Great Britain in 1988 by
Darton, Longman and Todd Ltd
89 Lillie Road, London SW6 1UD

Originally published in Dutch
by Lannoo in 1987 under the title
Brieven aan Marc

ISBN 0 232 51771 1

British Library Cataloguing in Publication Data

Nouwen, Henri J. M. (Henri Josef Machiel), *1932–*
    Letters to Marc about Jesus.
    1. Jesus Christ
    I. Title
    232

    ISBN 0–232–51771–1

Phototypeset by Input Typesetting Ltd, London SW19 8DR
Printed and bound by Anchor Brendon Ltd, Tiptree Essex

Contents

Preface

Some years ago, Herman Pijfers, a publisher friend of mine, asked me: 'Why don't you, for once, write a book in Dutch?' My answer at the time was: 'I've been living in the United States for so long and been in my own country so seldom that I feel no longer in a position to sense the mental climate in the Netherlands fairly or to say anything about it.' To this Herman came back with: 'Even so, write some letters, based on your personal situation, to a Dutch person to whom you really would like to convey something about the life of the spirit.' It was that simple, but fascinating, proposition that touched off these letters to Marc.

Marc van Campen is my sister's son, now nineteen years of age. When I asked him whether he might feel inclined to share the task of writing a 'book of letters' about the spiritual life, he turned out to be keen on it and promised his full co-operation. After that, it was some while before I could find time and quiet enough to begin writing; but when I did, at last get down to it, writing letters to Marc became such a source of inspiration for me that it proved easy to keep going.

So these are not letters which turned out, in retrospect, to be worth publishing. They were written with publication in mind. I make a point of this because it explains their style and tone. From the beginning, and despite the fact that these letters were, indeed, written for Marc, I had in mind a readership far wider than those of his age and upbringing. That may be why the 'epistolary' aspect has here and there gone by the board. Still it would not have been possible to write these texts at all, had Marc not been open to receiving them as an interested and critical party. From beginning to end he was the centre of my attention.

In the course of writing I became aware that I was engaged not only in telling Marc what I thought about Jesus and the meaning of our existence, but also in rediscovering Jesus and the meaning of my existence for myself. When I began these letters I had no precise idea as to how I should write about the spiritual life. I was often surprised at the way places where I was staying, events that were happening in the world and people whom I met were providing me with new ideas and new perspectives. These letters, then, have come to be the 'log' of a spiritual journey which I want to explain to Marc and to others besides. Although my initial intention was to write something helpful to Marc himself, it soon became evident that my main concern was to convey to him the enthusiasm I myself was feeling about my own discoveries. The letters in this book witness first and foremost, therefore, to my personal dealing with the life of faith. It was in that spirit also that Marc himself has received and valued them.

The original plan had been to record Marc's reactions as well. I eventually dropped that idea because it suited me better to use his reactions which were often requests for clarification in my reworking of the text. That made it possible to achieve a greater degree of internal unity and clarity in the text.

I am especially grateful to Herman Pijfers and to Marc for the part they have played in the writing of this book. Without them it would never have seen the light of day. I would also like to thank Mrs B. van Breemen for her secretarial assistance, Pieter Janssens and Margreet Stelling for their stylistic corrections and Lieven Sercu for being of such great help to me on the editorial side.

I very much hope that those who are asking themselves what it means to lead a spiritual life will be helped a little by this book.

LETTER 1

Jesus: the Heart of Our Existence

Tuesday, 11th February 1986

My dear Marc,

Well now, I've got round to it at last. It must be a year or so since I promised to write you some letters about the spiritual life. Over the past twelve months you've reminded me frequently of my promise. 'When are those letters of yours going to arrive?' It was difficult to get down to it because there always seemed to be something more urgent to attend to. However, if I were to let my life be taken over by what is urgent, I might very well never get around to what is essential. It's so easy to spend your whole time being preoccupied with urgent matters and never starting to live, really to live.

But is writing letters to you essential? Of course not, at least in the usual sense of the word. Even without any letters from me you have two dear parents, a lovely sister, a caring brother, a comfortable home, good food, a congenial school and plenty of relaxation. You're well looked after, in good health, and intelligent. At eighteen you've already seen a good deal of the world: France, Germany, Switzerland, Italy and the United States. You've also got plenty of hobbies: stamp collecting, filming, music (classical and modern), Egyptian art, and

1

lots to talk about. You've not only got a very inquiring mind, but you're also very gifted. There's really very little you can't do or can't acquire. So why do you need any letters from me?

When we spoke together about these letters, you said that you really did need them. That need, I think, is partly a consequence of your stay in the USA. When you attended that summer course at Concord, New Hampshire, and saw young men and women, as intelligent as yourself, who were genuinely concerned with religion in their lives, it raised some new questions in your mind. You asked yourself: 'What do I really believe? What kind of role does the Church play in my life? Who is Christ for me? Does the Eucharist make sense to me?' All those questions were more or less mixed up together; but it was clear that a new area had been opened up within you, and asked for your attention. You might say that in the last year or so a new need has been brought to birth inside you, the need, in the midst of everything you have and are doing, to look for the meaning and purpose of your life.

You yourself know that if you keep fit, if nothing goes wrong, if no war breaks out and so on, then you probably won't have much trouble in becoming a prosperous lawyer or a well-heeled business man. I haven't forgotten what you said to me in Boston: that you would probably come back to America later on to make a career. When I pointed out that a lot of people in America fail to make it, you replied with considerable self-confidence: 'Not the clever ones!' So you're evidently not worried about your financial prospects. Still, you're asking yourself: 'Even if I am a big success, so what?'

It may actually be your self-assurance that allows you to raise frankly the questions about the meaning of your life. A lot of people have to expend so much energy on overcoming their low opinion of themselves that they seldom get round to asking about the purpose of their existence. And if they do, it is often out of fear.

It's not like that for you. For you the question has a different significance because many problems, of which other people are intensely aware, are scarcely problems at all for you. Invariably, you sail through your homework and still get high marks for it. You're good at sports, have good friends and many interests. Everything comes easily for you. That is why, I think, you have room and time for asking yourself questions which to many of your class-mates seem irrelevant. Your American experience has given you the confidence to pose these questions quite directly and not bother about what your friends are going to think. In that sense your self-assurance would seem to be an advantage where the development of a spiritual life is concerned. For it is indeed the life of the spirit that we are dealing with here: that is what these letters must be about. Now, if you set out to confront issues that affect the meaning of your life, you can't adopt an approach based purely on reason. Questions about the meaning of your life affect your whole person. They are connected not only with the way you think and act, but also, and even more so, with the way you are a human being, and with the bond between you and everything that is.

Living spiritually is more than living physically, intellec-tually or emotionally. It embraces all that: but it is larger, deeper and wider. It concerns the core of your humanity. It's possible to lead a very wholesome, emotionally rich and 'sensible' life without being a spiritual person: that is, without knowledge or personal experience of the terrain where the meaning and goal of our human existence are hidden.

The spiritual life has to do with the heart of existence. I find the word 'heart' a good word. I don't mean by it the seat of our feelings as opposed to the seat of our thoughts. By 'heart' I mean the centre of our being, the 'place' where we are most ourselves, where we are most human, where we are most real. In that sense the heart is the focus of the spiritual life. I shall have more to say about that later on as well; but here and now I want to familiarize you with the word 'heart' because, for me, it is such an important word in the life of the spirit. There are times when I would like to substitute the expression, 'life of the heart' for 'the spiritual life'; but that smacks of sentimentality, and so I shall stick to the more traditional 'spiritual', as long as you realize that 'spiritual' is not the opposite of physical or emotional or intellectual. I haven't yet found a good word for the opposite of 'spiritual', but the 'un-spiritual' is that which does not affect the heart of our being, but remains on the surface. It belongs to the margins of existence rather than to its core.

There are many contexts for discussions about the 'spiritual life'. Buddhists, Hindus, Muslims are all living a spiritual life. Even people who see themselves as non-religious can have a profound spiritual life. However, when I write to you about the spiritual life, I do so as a Christian whose experience is that of living his Christianity in union with the Catholic tradition. For me, this is the sole possibility, in as much as it's only as a Catholic Christian that I know the spiritual life, to some extent, from the inside. And I want to write only about what I myself have lived out and lived through.

I want to give you a taste of the richness of life as a Christian, as I know it, experience it, and continue to discover it. I really do believe that I have something of importance to tell you and I am very happy that I can do so. It is good to be able to set what is most precious to me before someone who is happy to listen and who is also ready to take a very personal interest in it.

As you know, I'm thirty-six years older than you. When I was your age, I was at the Aloysius College in The Hague. At the time I found it very difficult to study, much more difficult than you do. I was a keen Scout and then a Rover. You probably find that hard to imagine. I used to attend daily Mass and was a diligent altar-boy. In that, too, our backgrounds differ. Along with other fellow students intending to become priests, I belonged to a group dedicated to self-examination with much discussion of prayer. This must sound strange to you now. Despite all the differences between those times and the present, the question of the spiritual life is no less relevant. The difference is that you don't have the support that I did. You have to face the question alone and must make a concerted effort to grapple with it on your own. It's not forced on you. For me it has been a life-long preoccupation.

Back in 1957 when I was ordained, I may have thought I knew what it was to live spiritually. If that's what I thought then, I certainly don't think so now. My studies in psychology at Nijmegen and my years spent teaching in the Netherlands, the United States and Latin America have taught me that raising questions about the spiritual life leads more to a new way of living than to a new way of thinking. These questions have to be lived rather than developed intellectually. I have tried to live them myself in various ways: with Catholics and Protestants, with Christians and humanists, with radical revolutionaries and traditional patriots, with the resentful and the resigned, with rich and poor, with the healthy and the sick. Time after time I've learned something new and discovered how much more there is to live.

In every phase of my search I've discovered also that Jesus Christ stands at the centre of my seeking. If you were to ask me point-blank: 'What does it mean to you to live spiritually?' I would have to reply: 'Living with Jesus at the centre.'

There are always countless questions, problems, discussions and difficulties that demand one's attention.

Despite this, when I look back over the last thirty years of my life, I can say that, for me, the person of Jesus has come to be more and more important. Specifically, this means that what matters increasingly is getting to know Jesus and living in solidarity with him. There was a time when I got so immersed in problems of Church and society that my whole life had become a sort of drawn-out, wearisome discussion. Jesus had been pushed into the background or had himself become just another problem. Fortunately, it hasn't stayed that way. Jesus has stepped out in front again, so to speak, and asked me: 'And you, who do you say that I am?' It has become clearer to me than ever that my personal relationship with Jesus is the heart of my existence.

It is about Jesus, above all, that I want to write to you in these letters and I want to to do so in a personal way. I don't want to lecture you about Jesus, but to tell you about him as I have come to know him. I am not trying to avoid the many questions about religion, Church, life today, war and peace, poverty and wealth, which you and I raise; but I do want to subordinate them to the question: 'Who is Jesus for you and for me?' So, what I intend is to start from my conviction that Jesus is the heart of my existence and, on that basis, to take a broad look at the world we live in. In doing so these letters can also help me to intensify my own experience of being a Christian and so prepare me for the Feast of the Resurrection which we shall be celebrating in forty days time, when Easter comes.

I do hope that with this letter we are on to something really good.

My warmest greeting to you,

Henri

LETTER 2

Jesus: the God Who Sets Us Free

Thursday, 13th February 1986

My dear Marc,

At the moment I'm in Freiburg-im-Breisgau, a charming little town in south Germany, completely rebuilt after the big air raid of 27th November 1944. As luck would have it, or thanks to instructions given to the officer commanding the bomber squadron, the beautiful cathedral remained almost undamaged. The Münster's slender tower stands like a resplendent jewel at the heart of the town and gives you a feeling of reassurance. Every time I visit this cathedral church I feel that much more centred and serene. The simple thought that construction on this church began in the year 1200 and went on until 1513 is reason enough to calm down and not behave as though everything has to be wrapped up this very afternoon. Freiburg today is a quiet, altogether peaceful little place. Everything runs like clockwork. The people are friendly, the shops full, the streets clean, the trains run on time, and you can see that no one goes short of anything. As there isn't much industry, the town has kept its intimate and homely character. This is reinforced by the way the centre has been reconstructed. Water burbles along the runnels laid down in the streets. Cars aren't admitted;

only a few colourful trams. In the evening, the finest buildings are floodlit; and from the open tower of the Münster there streams a warm, amber glow. It makes for a very inviting atmosphere.

Walking around here like this, I have the feeling that this world of ours must be all right. Things are going well. But you yourself know that Freiburg doesn't tell the whole story. The papers are full of dictator 'Baby Doc' Duvalier's flight from Haiti and of the violent disorder accompanying the elections in the Philippines. From everywhere there comes news of violence and oppression. The new leader in Uganda, Yoweri Museveni shows newsmen the mass graves of the victims of his predecessor, Milton Obote. Museveni claims that between 1980 and 1985 some 200,000 people in his country were murdered. You have only to think now of South Africa, Northern Ireland, Iran and Iraq, Central America, and many other places in the world to know beyond a doubt that the peace and quiet of Freiburg tell a good deal less than half the truth.

I'm also reminded of this by two priests with whom I have breakfast every morning. One is a refugee from Czechoslovakia, and the other is a Croat. Their stories confirm what the newspapers tell us in all sorts of ways; for most people freedom is a dream. It's a lot easier to find evidence of oppression in this world than of freedom. And from what I know of history I get the impression that it has never been much different.

I'm mentioning all this to help you appreciate the first story I want to tell you about Jesus. It's the story of Cleopas and his friend who, with heavy hearts, had set out on the road from Jerusalem to Emmaus. They were going home, disillusioned, dejected and downcast. We don't know much about these two friends, but Luke in his Gospel intimates quite clearly how they felt: beaten and oppressed. For a long time past, the Romans had been masters in their country; there was little genuine freedom and, as anyone would be, they were impatient to be free. When they came to know Jesus, their hopes were raised that this man from Nazareth would be able to give them the freedom they had been looking forward to for so long. But it had all come to nothing. The Jesus of whom they had expected so much had been arrested, condemned to death, and crucified by the Romans. Everything was just as it had been before: a life in which you could be picked up at any moment and put in jail. Again, freedom has not come. Cleopas and his friend had lost heart. In their despair they were making their way back home. It was not a way of hope. It was a cheerless way, a despairing way.

It will not be easy for you to identify with these two men. You've had no experience of being oppressed. I can still remember vaguely what it is like. I was thirteen when the Second World War ended. I can still recall the infamous hunger-winter and the victorious entry of the Canadians in May 1945. I've had personal experience of the difference between 'being occupied' and 'being free', and so I know what a privileged individual I've been since 1945. For you, being oppressed is an unknown experience. Nevertheless, you are, I think, somewhat able to put yourself in the shoes of people who above all else long to be completely and utterly free, and you are able to understand how they must feel.

Jesus falls in with the two men, but they fail to recognize him. What does he do? First he listens to their sorry tale. He tags on to them in a very personal, you might say intimate, fashion. He enters right into their sense of disappointment. He shares their feelings with them. He is prepared to be where they are.

Here you have to imagine what had happened to Jesus himself. He had been hideously tortured to death and then buried. People often talk about Jesus as though his death had been followed immediately by his resurrection but that's not what is reported to us by the gospels. Jesus lay in the tomb for three days. That means not only that he had been like many people today the victim of oppression, but also that his body like everyone else's proceeded to decay. When Lazarus had been lying in the tomb for four days, his sister Martha said to Jesus: 'He's stinking already.' The grave is a place of putrefaction. Jesus lay in the tomb for three days; and there his body putrefied. I mention this because decomposition is surely the most telling symbol of man's desperation. Whatever we do or say, however learned we are, however many our friends or great our wealth, soon – in ten, thirty, fifty, seventy years' time – we shall rot. That's why we are so deeply affected by life's disappointments and setbacks. They remind us that, sooner or later, everything decays. Despair is our inner conviction that, in the end, it is utterly impossible to stop anything from coming to nothing.

Left with the impression that their great expectations had once again been shattered, Cleopas and his friend were grief-stricken. Yet again, it had become painfully clear to them just how meaningless their lives really were. They had already caught a whiff of the decay afflicting their own lives. So it was with bowed heads that they were making for home. It wasn't just their adventure with Jesus that was over, everything else had come to nothing in the end.

So when Jesus falls in with these two dejected men, he knows very well what is in their hearts. He knows from experience what human despair is. He knows death and the tomb; he knows what it means to be mortal. Cleopas and his friend must, I think, have perceived that this stranger was really no stranger at all. He understood them too well to remain strange to them for long. They saw that this man was not going to offer them easy words of comfort. When it is Jesus' turn to speak, he speaks with authority. An authority based not on power but on personal experience. That's why they listen to him so attentively.

What does Jesus tell them? Not that death and the dissolution of life are unreal. Nor that their yearning for freedom is unreal. No: in what he says he takes seriously not only death and dissolution but their longing for freedom as well. He tells them that the Jesus on whom they had pinned all their hopes, the Jesus who was indeed dead and buried, this Jesus is alive. He tells them that for the Jesus whom they had admired so much, death and dissolution have become the way to liberation. And he says this in such a way that they sense in their innermost selves that his way can become their way too.

As Jesus was talking to them, they experienced in their hearts something new. It was as if their hearts were burning with a flame that came not from without but from within. Jesus had kindled in them something for which they had no words but which was so authentic, so real, that it overcame their depression. Jesus had not said: 'It isn't nearly as bad as you think.' He had said something entirely new: 'The most tragic, the most painful, the most hopeless circumstances can become the way to the liberation you long for most of all.'

It's very difficult for you and me to grasp much of this. In fact, it goes against logic. You and I as rational people say: 'Death is death. Death and all that approaches it or leads to it must be avoided at all costs. The further away we can stay from death and everything connected to it – pain, illness, war, oppression, poverty, hunger and so on – the better for us.' That's a normal, spontaneous human attitude. Jesus makes us see human existence from a quite different angle, one that is beyond the reach of our ordinary common sense.

Jesus makes us see existence in terms of his own experience that life is stronger and greater than death and dissolution. It's only with our hearts that we can understand this, and Luke doesn't write: 'Then it dawned on them' or 'Then they saw the light'. No, he says: 'Their hearts burned within them.' The burning heart revealed something completely new to Cleopas and his friend. At the centre of their being, of their humanity, something was generated that could disarm death and rob despair of its power; something much more than a new outlook on things, a new confidence or a new joy in living; something that can be described only as a new life or a new spirit. Nowadays we would say: 'In their hearts the spiritual life had begun'; but it's better not to use these terms at this point. Otherwise, we shall stray too far from the actual story and there's too much still to be told.

When the three men reached Emmaus, so much had happened between them that the two companions were unwilling to let the stranger go. Between these two and Jesus there had arisen a bond which had given them new hope, even though they scarcely knew why. They felt that this unknown individual had given them something new. They didn't want to go indoors without him. So they said: 'Stay with us. It's just about evening; and the day is as good as over.' Luke, in his account, even says that they implored him to be their guest. Jesus accepted the invitation and went in with them.

And now there happens something which, for you and me, is of major significance. It touches the very core of the spiritual life. When they sit down to eat, Jesus takes some bread, speaks a blessing over it, and breaks it and offers it to them. And as he does so, they know suddenly and with unshakeable certainty that this stranger is Jesus, the same Jesus who had been put to death and laid in a tomb. But at the precise moment this certainty is given to them, he becomes invisible to them.

So much is going on here that it's difficult to get its full significance across to you, and so I shall limit myself to what is, for me, a very crucial aspect of this incident. What matters here is that the moment Cleopas and his friend recognized Jesus in the breaking of bread, his bodily presence was no longer required as a condition for their new hope. You might say that the bond between them and the stranger had become so intimate that everything strange about him vanishes, and, in the most literal sense, he becomes their bosom friend. So close does he come to them that they no longer need a bodily manifestation in order to hope. They realize now that the new life born in them as they talked with him on the road will stay with them and give them the strength to return to Jerusalem and tell the other people why it isn't true that 'it's all over'. That's why Luke reports that they went off straightaway to tell Jesus' other friends about their experience.

Are you beginning to see what I'm getting at? Cleopas and his friend had become different people. Because they had experienced for themselves that the Jesus whom they had mourned for was alive and closer to them than ever, their hearts were born again, and their inner life was made radically new. That's something quite different from taking on board a new conviction or acquiring a new outlook on things or undergoing a change of opinion. Something much more profound than that had happened to these two. The Jesus they had seen had come not only into their home, but into their hearts as well, so that they were able then to share in the new life he had won through his death and disintegration.

What you see here is a process of fundamental liberation. Because Jesus joined them, the two men who walked to Emmaus made a spiritual journey too. When they first set out, liberation still meant shaking off the Roman yoke. They had hoped that Jesus would help them, and they were deeply dismayed when their great hero, their liberator, was put to death. But then, when

Jesus offered them the bread and their eyes were opened, they became conscious of a freedom they had never thought possible. It was a freedom which they could hardly anticipate because they had no conception of it. It was a freedom unknown to them and, therefore, beyond their asking. It was freedom that went much further and deeper than the freedom for which they had hoped and dreamed; a freedom that invaded their hearts to the very depths; a freedom that no earthly power, Roman or Jewish, could take from them. It was a freedom of the spirit: a freedom from any specific political, economic or social expectations in the future, a freedom to follow the Lord now, anywhere, even if it should mean suffering.

Let me take these thoughts about the freedom Jesus gives to Cleopas and his friend a little further. The better you understand that spiritual freedom and get the feel of it for yourself, the greater the chance that you will come to discover who Jesus is. In the present century a number of people have written about this spiritual freedom: Dietrich Bonhoeffer, in his book *Letters and Papers from Prison*; Etty Hillesum, in *Etty: A Diary 1941–43*; Titus Brandsma, in his letters from a Dutch jail. Amid the most frightful forms of oppression and violence these people discovered within themselves a place where no one had power over them, where they were wholly free. Although very different from one another, they had in common an awareness of spiritual freedom that enabled them to stand on their own two feet in the world, without being manipulated by that world. Their freedom was such that they had even overcome, to a great extent, the fear of death. They knew in their heart of hearts that those who might be able to destroy their bodies would never be able to deprive them of their freedom. Jesus himself spoke of that freedom when he told his disciples: 'Do not be afraid of those who kill the body but cannot kill the soul.'

What I personally find so fascinating is that this *spiritual* freedom is something quite different from a *spiritualized* freedom. The freedom Jesus gives doesn't imply that oppressors can go on oppressing, that the poor can stay poor and the hungry can stay hungry since we are now, in a spiritual respect, free. A true spiritual freedom that touches the heart of our being in all its humanity must take effect in every sphere: physical, psychical, social and, in a global sense, terrestrial. It is meant to be everywhere visible; but the core of this spiritual freedom doesn't depend on the manner in which it is made visible. A sick, mentally handicapped or oppressed person can still be spiritually free, even if that freedom cannot as yet manifest itself in every area of life.

I became sharply aware of this when I visited Nicaragua. In one small village, Jalapa, I talked with the women whose husbands or sons had been brutally murdered by the so-called Contras. These women knew all too well that the Contras were being backed by the United States; and yet there was no detectable trace of hatred or vindictiveness in them. They remembered the words of Jesus on the cross, 'Father, forgive them; they do not know what they are doing', and were ready, like Jesus, to pray for their enemies to be forgiven.

When I was with them, I sensed their deep spiritual freedom. Amid all the oppression no one had been able to deprive them of that. Their hearts had remained free, and their indescribable suffering had not broken their spirits. For me, that was an unforgettable experience. There, on the border between Nicaragua and Honduras, I saw something of that same freedom which Cleopas and his friend knew after they had recognized Jesus and admitted him into their hearts.

Freedom belongs to the core of the spiritual life; not just the freedom which releases us from forces that want to oppress us, but the freedom also to forgive others, to serve them and to form a new bond of fellowship with

15

them. In short, the freedom to love and to work for a free world.

I should really leave it at that. But I still want to tell you something else concerning Luke's Emmaus story, something which has quite concrete consequences for your day-to-day life. Something that will bring the event a bit closer to you.

The story was written when the first Christian congregations had already been formed. So it speaks to us not only about Jesus and the spiritual life, but also about life in the very early Church. In fact, it was written within the context of a believing community and its lived experience. That gives the story a whole new dimension. It tells us something about the different aspects of communal worship: owning up to our confusion, depression, despair and guilt; listening with an open heart to the Word of God; gathering around the table to break the bread and so to acknowledge the presence of Jesus; and going out again into the world to make known to others what we have learned and experienced in our lives. You've probably seen already that these are the various components of a eucharistic celebration. It's there that you find confession of guilt, proclamation and exposition of the Word, partaking of the Lord's Supper and being sent out into the world. Thus, you can say that each time you celebrate the Eucharist you once again make the journey from Jerusalem to Emmaus and back. You can say, too, that each time you celebrate the Eucharist you are able to achieve a bit more spiritual freedom. Freedom from the subjugating powers of this world – powers that forever try to entice you to become rich and popular – and freedom to love friend and foe.

So here you are, very nearly back on home ground after all. You've often asked me about the meaning of the Eucharist. Insofar as you get to know Jesus, you will begin to understand better the significance of the Eucharist. This letter will, I hope, help you to appreciate the connection.

This has turned out to be a long letter. I have worked on it, though not without a good deal of joy, for quite some time. It's now half past five on a Saturday afternoon, and I just want to get back into the centre of Freiburg once more to visit the cathedral. It's always very quiet on a Saturday afternoon in the square. By the time I get there, it will be dark, and that warm, amber light will be glowing again through the spire. I wish you were here so we could go together. That can't be, alas! So I'm enclosing a few postcards. They will give you some idea at any rate.

Greetings and love to your parents, and to Frédérique and Reinier.

Till next time,

Henri

LETTER 3

Jesus: the Compassionate God

Monday, 17 February 1986

My dear Marc,

Yesterday I went with some friends to Colmar; Colmar is a French town in Alsace, by car an hour or less from Freiburg. We went there to take a look at the Isenheimer Altar. You probably have heard about it already, and may even have seen it. For me it proved to be a very profound experience.

The Isenheimer Altar was painted between 1513 and 1515 for the chapel at the hospital for plague victims in the small village of Isenheim, not far from Colmar. The artist was a man of such a retiring disposition, some say very melancholic as well, that historians are still unable to agree as to who he actually was. According to most authorities, Matthias Grünewald was the creator of this masterpiece in which the whole pictorial art of the late Middle Ages is summed up and brought to its highest point. Many people think this work is not only the most spectacular, but also the most moving altarpiece ever made. It is a multiple series of panels.

The front panel depicts Jesus' death on the cross. On the second Grünewald has painted the Annunciation, the birth of Jesus and his resurrection. On the third, which

18

consists of two panels on each side of a group of sculpted figures, you can see the temptations of St Anthony and his visit to the hermit Paul.

Although I had read two booklets by Wilhelm Nyssen in preparation for our visit to this altar, the reality surpassed any description or reproduction. When I saw the body of Jesus on the cross, tortured, emaciated and covered with abscesses, I had an inkling of the reaction of the plague-stricken and dying sufferers in the sixteenth century. On this altar, they saw their God, with the same suppurating ulcers as their own, and it made them realize with a shock what the Incarnation really meant. They saw solidarity, compassion, forgiveness and unending love brought together in this one suffering figure. They saw that, in their mortal anguish, they had not been left on their own.

But they saw too, when the front panel was opened out, that the tortured body of Jesus, born of Mary, had not only died for them but, also for them, had risen gloriously from death. The same ulcerated body which they saw hanging dead on the cross exudes now a dazzling light, and rises upward in divine splendour – a splendour which is also in store for us.

The two Anthony panels, on each side of the dramatic statuary, reminded the plague-ridden sufferers that sharing in the divine glory of Jesus demands a readiness to share in his temptations as well. Anthony was the patron of the monastic order that nursed the plague victims, and his life showed, without any cheap sentimentality, that those who would follow Jesus are bound to have a narrow and frequently rocky road to tread.

I remained at the Isenheimer Altar for three hours or more. During those three hours I learned more about suffering and resurrection than from days and days of reading. The crucified and risen Christ of Matthias Grünewald is carved so deeply into my memory and imagination

Matthias Grünewald, *The Crucifixion* from the Isenheimer Altar
(Unterlinden Museum, Colmar. Photo: O. Zimmermann)

now that wherever I go or stay I can call him to mind. I know now, in a completely new way, that if I am to succeed in fully living my life, in all its painful yet glorious moments, I must remain united to Jesus.

As we drove back through the vine-covered hills of the 'Kaiserstuhl', I also came to understand better what Jesus meant when he said to his friends: 'I am the vine, you are the branches. Whoever remains in me, with me in him, bears fruit in plenty; for cut off from me you can do nothing.'

Remarkably enough, I'd already made up my mind last week to write to you this week about the suffering and resurrection of Christ. At that time I hadn't yet seen the Isenheimer Altar. Now I have a feeling that I had to see it in order to find the words I need for this letter.

The record of the suffering and resurrection of Jesus forms the kernel of the 'good news' which Jesus' disciples

Matthias Grünewald, *The Resurrection* from the Isenheimer Altar
(Unterlinden Museum, Colmar. Photo: O. Zimmermann)

intended to make known to the world. Jesus is the Lord who has suffered, died and was buried, and rose again on the third day. Everyone had to know about that. These were the 'glad tidings' and so they still are. You could say that everything else the four Gospels have to say about Jesus is intended to bring out the full significance of his suffering, death and resurrection.

When I saw the Isenheimer Altar yesterday, this became clear to me again. Without the death and resurrection of Jesus the gospel is a beautiful tale about an exceptionally saintly person, a tale that might inspire good thoughts and great deeds; but there are other stories of that sort. The gospel is, first and foremost, the story of the death and resurrection of Jesus, and that story also forms the heart of the spiritual life. Grünewald understood this and wanted to make it plain to the dying men and women of his time.

It won't be easy to write to you about the death and resurrection of Jesus in a way that would affect you deeply as you read it. True, you've had scarcely any proper instruction in religion and have taken only a sporadic interest in the gospel, but the story of Jesus' death and resurrection is such a familiar part of the milieu in which you've grown up that it can hardly surprise, astound, or shock any more. You're more likely to say: 'Oh yes. I know about that: let's talk about something else.' Yet somehow I have to alert you to the truth that what this is all about (the suffering, death, and resurrection of Jesus) is the most fundamental, the most far-reaching event ever to occur in the course of history. If you don't see and feel that for yourself, then the gospel can be, at most, interesting, but it can never renew your heart and make you a reborn human being. And rebirth is what it's all about – a radical liberation that sets us free from the power of death and empowers us to love fearlessly. When I saw Grünewald's painting of the tortured, naked body of

Jesus, I realized anew that the cross isn't just a beautiful piece of art decorating the living rooms and restaurants of Freiburg; it's the sign of the most radical transformation in our manner of thinking, feeling, and living. Jesus' death on the cross has changed everything. What is the most spontaneous human response to suffering and death? For me, the words that spring immediately to mind are: preventing, avoiding, denying, shunning, keeping clear of and ignoring. All of these words indicate that suffering and death don't fit into our programme for living. We react to them as uninvited, undesirable, and unwelcome interlopers, and we want to show them the door as soon as we can. If we ourselves get sick, our primary concern is to get better as quickly as possible. If that doesn't happen, then we try to persuade ourselves or each other that it may not be as bad as it looks and to convince one another, often against all odds, that everything will be all right again. If, nevertheless, death does come, we are often surprised, taken aback, deeply disappointed, or even angry.

Fortunately, efforts are being made to bring about a change in this attitude and to take a more realistic view of suffering and death; but my own experience has been that, for most people, these are still the chief enemies of life. They really ought not to exist. We must try, somehow, to get them under control as well as we can and, if that doesn't work the first time, we must try to do better the second time.

There are many sick people who don't have much understanding of their sickness, and often they die without ever having given much thought to their death. About a year ago a friend of mine died of cancer. Six months before his death, it was already obvious that he hadn't long to live. Even so, it was very difficult to prepare him properly for his death. He was so hedged around with tubes and hoses and busy nurses, that one got the

23

impression that he had to be kept alive at any price. I am not saying that anyone did anything wrong, but I do say that so much attention was given to keeping him alive that there was hardly time to prepare him for death.

The result of this for us is that we no longer pay much attention to the dead. We do little to remember them, that is, to make them a part of our interior life. How often do you visit your grandmother's grave? How often do your mother and I visit the graves of our deceased grandparents, uncles, aunts, and friends? In fact, we behave as though they no longer belong to us, as though we have nothing more to do with them. They no longer have any real influence on our lives. Not only have they gone from us physically, but they have also left the world of our thoughts and feelings.

Jesus' attitude to suffering and death was quite different. For him, they were realities he encountered with his eyes wide open. Actually, his whole life was a conscious preparation for them. Jesus doesn't commend suffering and death as desirable things; but he does speak of them as something we ought not to repudiate, avoid, or cover up.

On a number of occasions he foretold his own suffering and death. Quite soon after Jesus had commissioned his twelve disciples, he was already telling them: 'The Son of Man is destined to suffer grievously, to be rejected by the elders and chief priests and scribes and to be put to death, and to be raised up on the third day.' Not so long after, he repeated this prophecy with the words: 'You must have these words constantly in mind: The Son of Man is going to be delivered into the power of men.' That even in those days they wanted to ignore reality is surely evident from Peter's reaction. 'Then, taking him aside, Peter started to rebuke him. "Heaven preserve you, Lord," he said, "This must not happen to you." ' Jesus' reply is cutting. It would even appear that he regards

Peter's reaction as the most dangerous of all for those in quest of a truly spiritual life: 'Get behind me, Satan! You are an obstacle in my path, because you are thinking not as God thinks but as human beings do.' After that, he tells his disciples yet again, and very plainly, that a person wanting to lead a spiritual life cannot do so without the prospect of suffering and death. Living spiritually is made possible only through a direct, uncushioned confrontation with the reality of death. Just listen to what Jesus has to say: 'If anyone wants to be a follower of mine, let him renounce himself and take up his cross and follow me. Anyone who wants to save his life will lose it; but anyone who loses his life for my sake will find it.'

Finding new life through suffering and death: that is the core of the good news. Jesus has lived out that liberating way before us and has made it the great sign. Human beings are forever wanting to see signs: marvellous, extraordinary, sensational events that can distract them a little from hard reality. It isn't without reason that we keep on looking among the stars to see whether they are stars of earth or stars of heaven. We would like to see something marvellous, something exceptional, something that interrupts the ordinary life of every day. That way, if only for a moment, we can play at hide-and-seek. But to those who say to Jesus: 'Master, . . . we should like to see a sign from you,' he replies: 'It is an evil and unfaithful generation that asks for a sign! The only sign it will be given is the sign of the prophet Jonah. For as Jonah remained in the belly of the sea monster for three days and three nights, so will the Son of Man be in the heart of the earth for three days and three nights.'

From this you can see what the authentic sign is; not some sensational miracle but the suffering, death, burial, and resurrection of Jesus. The great sign, which can be understood only by those who are willing to follow Jesus, is the sign of Jonah, who also wanted to run away from

25

reality but was summoned back by God to fulfil his arduous task to the end. To look suffering and death straight in the face *and* to go through them oneself in the hope of a new God-given life: that is the sign of Jesus and of every human being who wishes to lead a spiritual life in imitation of him. It is the sign of the cross: the sign of suffering and death, but also of the hope for total renewal.

That's why Matthias Grünewald had the courage to confront the dying patients in the Isenheim hospital so directly with the terrible suffering of Jesus. He dared to show them what we all prefer to shut our eyes to because he believed that suffering and death no longer barred the way to the new life but had become, through Jesus, the way to it. If you look carefully, you see that the cross painted by Grünewald looks like a drawn bow with an arrow. That is in itself a sign of hope. The tortured body of Jesus is bound, so to speak, to an arrow pointing toward the new life.

So what, in concrete terms, are we to make of Jesus' suffering and death? In telling you the story of Cleopas and his friend, I wanted to show you that freedom is an essential aspect of the spiritual life. From the story of Jesus' suffering and death it will be clear to you now that compassion must be added to freedom. The spiritual life is a free life that becomes visible in compassion. I now want to help you to see and feel this more clearly.

God sent Jesus to make free persons of us. He has chosen compassion as the way to freedom. That is a great deal more radical than you might at first imagine. It means that God wanted to liberate us, not by removing suffering from us, but by sharing it with us. Jesus is God-who-suffers-with-us. Over time, the word 'sympathizing' has become a somewhat feeble way of expressing the reality of 'suffering with' someone. Nowadays, when someone says: 'I have sympathy for you,' it has a rather distant ring about it. The feeling, at least for me, is of someone looking down from above. The word's original meaning of 'suffering together with someone' has been partly lost. That's why I've opted for the word 'compassion'. It's warmer, more intimate, and closer. It's taking part in the suffering of the other, being totally a fellow-human-being in suffering.

God's love, which Jesus wants to make us see, is shown to us by his becoming a partner and a companion in our suffering, thus enabling us to turn it into a way to liberation. You're probably familiar with the questions most frequently raised by people who find it difficult or impossible to believe in God. How can God really love the world when he permits all that frightful suffering? If God really loves us, why doesn't he put an end to war, poverty, hunger, sickness, persecution, torture, and all the other misery that we see everywhere? If God cares about me personally, why am I in such bad shape? . . . why do I always feel so lonely? . . . why am I still without a job? . . . why do I feel my existence to be so pointless?

I've been occupied continually with these questions myself, especially since I got to know the poverty that exists in South and Central America and saw how innocent Indians are kidnapped, tortured and killed in the most cruel fashion.

At the same time it was there too that I found the beginning of an answer! I discovered that the victims of poverty and oppression were often more deeply convinced of God's love than we are and that the question of the why of suffering was raised less by those people who had tasted suffering themselves than by us who had merely heard and read about it. Seldom have I seen so much trust in God as among the poor and oppressed Indians of South and Central America. While it seems to be getting more and more difficult for a lot of people in the Netherlands who have become increasingly well off during the last few years, to have a sense of the nearness of God in their day-to-day lives, many men and women in Latin America, whose suffering can be read on their faces, are filled with the Spirit when they tell how God gives them hope and courage.

You will appreciate, of course, the deep impression this has made on me. I've gradually come to see that these people have learned to know Jesus as the God who suffers with them. For them, the suffering and dying Jesus is the most convincing sign that God really loves them very much and does not leave them in the lurch. He is their companion in suffering. If they are poor, they know that Jesus was poor too; if they are afraid, they know that Jesus also was afraid; if they are beaten, they know that Jesus too was beaten; and if they are tortured to death, well then, they know that Jesus suffered the same fate. For these people, Jesus is the faithful friend who treads with them the lonely road of suffering and brings them consolation. He is with them in solidarity. He knows them, understands them, and clasps them to himself in their moments of greatest pain.

The statues of Jesus that I saw in the churches of San Pedro in Lima, and in those of Santiago at the lake of Atitlán in Guatemala, present an exhausted man, scourged, crowned with thorns, and covered with wounds. I often found it horrible to look at; but for the Peruvians and Guatemalan Indians, this broken human being was their greatest source of hope.

Perhaps all of this seems a bit remote, yet you and I too have experiences that make us sensitive to the compassion of Jesus. A real friend isn't someone who can solve all your problems or who has an answer to every question. No, a real friend is someone who doesn't walk off when there are no solutions or answers, but sticks by you and remains faithful to you. It often turns out that the one who gives us the most comfort is not the person who says: 'Do this, say that, go there,' but the one who, even if there is no good advice to give, says; 'Whatever happens, I'm your friend; you can count on me.' The older you become, the more you discover that your joy and happiness depend on such friendships. The great secret in life is that suffering, which often seems to be so unbearable, can become, through compassion, a source of new life and new hope.

God has become human so as to be able, in all completeness, to live with us, suffer with us and die with us. We have found in Jesus a fellow human being who is so completely one with us that not a single weakness, pain or temptation has remained foreign to him. Precisely because Jesus is God and without any sin, he is able to experience our sinful, broken human condition so thoroughly that we may say he knows us better than we know ourselves and loves us more than we love ourselves. No one else, however well disposed, is ever in a position to be with us so completely that we feel ourselves to be understood and loved without limit. We humans remain too self-centred to be able to forget ourselves fully for the other person's sake. But Jesus does give himself fully, he holds nothing back for himself, he wants to be with us in so total a fashion that we can never again feel alone.

Jesus is the compassionate God who comes so close to us in our weakness that we can turn to him without fear. The Letter to the Hebrews puts it in incomparably profound words: 'He has been put to the test in exactly the same way as ourselves, apart from sin. Let us, then, have no fear in approaching the throne of grace to receive mercy and to find grace when we are in need of help.'

I hope that you can grasp something of all this and take it to heart. In the end, I think it is only through prayer that you can come to understand it. When you stand before God, vulnerable as you are, and let him see all there is of you, you will begin gradually to experience for yourself what it means that God has sent Jesus to be, in all things, God-with-you. Then you will begin to know that, by becoming a human being in Jesus, God is offering you his divine life. Then you can ask yourself in a new way how you wish to conduct your own life.

In my previous letter, the key word was freedom. In this one it is compassion. When you come to see Jesus more and more as the compassionate God, you will begin increasingly to see your own life as one in which you yourself want to express that divine compassion. What can happen then is that you feel a deep longing grow within you to make your own life a life for others. The better you learn to know and love Jesus, the more you find yourself longing to lead your life in conformity with his. You already discovered some of that for yourself when you read Thomas à Kempis' *Imitation of Christ*. You observed then that it involved something quite radical but also very inviting. Living for other people in solidarity with the compassionate Jesus: that's what it means to live a spiritual life. In that way also you achieve true freedom.

Before I finish this letter I want to show, as in my previous letter, that the account of Jesus' suffering, death, and resurrection is not just a story about the past. Like the Emmaus story, it was written from within the Christian community. In this community the Eucharist was and is celebrated. That's why the account of the Last Supper belongs to the Passion story. It's there you read that before his suffering and death Jesus took the bread and the wine and said to his friends: 'This is my body which is given for you. Do this in memory of me.'

You've heard these words so often already that, for you, they no longer carry their full and proper weight. But consider what is taking place here. Jesus is saying: 'I want to give myself to you totally. As intimately as food and drink are united with your body, so would I be united with you. I don't want to keep anything for myself. I want to be eaten and drunk by you.' You could best translate Jesus' words, therefore, as; 'Eat me, drink me.' What you have to hear and feel in this is the completely self-giving love of Jesus. The suffering and death that follow the Last Supper are a way of making visible that self-giving love. The agony, the scourging, mocking, crowning with thorns, the crucifixion and death of Jesus allow us to see in the most drastic manner possible how utterly Jesus gives himself to us, when he says: 'Eat me, drink me.' In that sense, you might say that the account of the Passion makes plain to us what has already taken place at the Last Supper.

The Eucharist was and is the centre of the fellowship of those who put all their trust in Jesus. It was within the setting of the eucharistic celebration that the first Christians told to one another the story of Jesus' suffering and death. It was also from within this eucharistic community that the story was recorded by the gospel writers. This is so very important for you and me because we are able to celebrate the Eucharist day by day. With every celebration, the suffering, death, and resurrection of Jesus are made present. The best way to put it might be like this: every time you celebrate the Eucharist and receive the bread and wine, the body and blood of Jesus, his suffering and his death become a suffering and death for you. Passion becomes compassion, for you. You are incorporated into Jesus. You become part of his 'body' and in that most compassionate way are freed from your deepest solitude. Through the Eucharist you come to belong to Jesus in the most intimate way, to him who has suffered for you, died for you and rose again so that you may suffer, die and rise again with him.

Do you understand better now why Matthias Grünewald chose the altar at Isenheim as the appropriate place for his moving portrayal of Christ's suffering, death, and resurrection? He was showing these mortally sick people what it was that the Eucharist really gave them. They had no more need to endure their plague alone. They were incorporated into the suffering of Jesus, and so could trust also that they would be allowed to share in his resurrection.

I'm enclosing some photos of Grünewald's altar panels so that you can see and realize for yourself the meaning of God's compassion for us human beings.

I will leave it at that for now. There's so much more still to be said. As I was writing this letter, I became aware of how much I would have to restrict myself; but then, it is not necessary to get everything down on paper. In the end, I just want to get you to read the Bible and develop your spiritual life for yourself. My letters are only meant to spur you on a bit.

A friend of mine arrived yesterday from Boston to spend a few days' vacation with me. His name is Jonas. He arrived at the very moment I was writing to you about the prophet Jonah. Today we're going to look around Freiburg, and tomorrow we're off to the Black Forest; the day after that we go via Paris to Trosly, a small French village where I am staying until the end of August. So I shall send you my next letter from France and tell you something of my work and my life there.

Greetings and love to all the family.

Until next time,

Henri

LETTER 4

Jesus: the Descending God

Tuesday, 25th February 1986

My dear Marc,

So here I am, writing from France. My friend Jonas and I had a good journey, with a stop-off at Strasbourg. Along with two other priests I was invited to celebrate the holy Eucharist in the cathedral. It was an extraordinary experience to be able to look from the high altar into the majestic Gothic nave and watch the sunlight pouring in through the beautiful rose window. During his sermon, the preacher pointed to that huge round window of stained glass and said: 'It is a work of art made by human beings. But unless God's sun shines through it, we see nothing.'

The enormous cathedral impressed Jonas and me deeply. We felt at one with the many generations who have lived and prayed in Strasbourg. But now I'm 'home' again in Trosly, where everything is small and very unpretentious. Jonas has gone back to Boston, and I'm sitting here writing to you in the small but cosy room where I've been living since August.

In this letter, I want to speak to you about the love of God made visible by Jesus in his life. When I asked myself how I could best do this, I began to realize that my life here in this French village would be the most obvious starting point. Trosly, close to Compiègne, in northern France, is an undistinguished little place. It would never have occurred to me to come and spend a year here, were it not for the fact that in August 1964 a Canadian, Jean Vanier, purchased a small house here, invited two handicapped men to come and live with him and thus started a new community, which he called 'The Ark.' Now, in 1986, 'L'Arche' is known and loved in many countries.

Initially, all that Jean Vanier himself wanted was just to live in poverty with poor people. He had grown up in an aristocratic environment; from 1959 to 1967 his father was Governor-General of Canada. After serving five years in the navy Jean went on to study philosophy in Paris and then became assistant professor at St Michael's College at the University of Toronto. He was soon popular there, but success left him unsatisfied. He felt called to another kind of life: simpler, poorer, and more centred on prayer and commitment to service. He thought of becoming a priest; but shortly before his ordination he realized that Christ was asking something else of him. At first, he didn't know what the 'something else' was; but gradually, under the direction of the Dominican, Thomas Philippe, he realized that he was being asked to give up his career at the university and invite two mentally handicapped people, Raphael and Philippe, to live with him at home – thus beginning a very simple life in imitation of Jesus.

When he took these two men out of the institution and brought them to his 'Ark' in Trosly, he knew he had done something for which there could be no going back. Raphael and Philippe had no parents or family who could look after them. Sending them back to the institution from which they had been released was unthinkable. He was committed to these two mentally injured people for the rest of his life. He himself felt it to be a bond with the poor in spirit, a bond that demanded of him the loyalty of a lifetime.

In August of 1964, Jean Vanier had no other idea than to devote his whole life to Raphael and Philippe. Although he was deeply convinced to the dismay, at first, of his parents that he was being called to give up his very promising academic career for these two poor people – he knew little or nothing about caring for the handicapped. He relied on his intuition and the support and encouragement offered by his spiritual director, Thomas Philippe. However, when word of Jean Vanier's decision got out, young people from various countries began arriving in Trosly to help him. Quite contrary to what Jean had expected, his small 'Ark' household soon grew into a world-wide movement with homes for mentally handicapped people not only in Western Europe, but in Asia, Africa, and North America as well.

A few years ago, when I was still teaching at Yale University, Jean sent one of his co-workers to invite me, in the way of friendship, to get in touch with him. That was the first step of a journey of spiritual discovery which, eventually, made me decide to resign from the university and go to Trosly with the possibility of making 'L'Arche' my new home.

So here I am in my new surroundings. I may say that the contrast between my university life and my life here in L' Arche is greater than I realized at the outset. The contrast isn't so much between intelligent students and mentally handicapped people as in the 'ascending' style of the university and the 'descending' style of L'Arche. You might say that at Yale and Harvard they're principally interested in upward mobility, whereas here they believe in the importance of downward mobility. That's the radical difference, and I notice in myself how difficult it is to change direction on the ladder.

When Jean Vanier moved from Toronto to Trosly, he made a radical change of direction in his life. He renounced a career that would take him higher and higher up the ladder of success for a vocation that brought him down to the level of the poor, the weak, the sick and those in distress. It has become very clear to me now that the further you descend, the more your eyes are opened to the brokenness of our humanity.

I said at the beginning of this letter that I wanted to write to you about the love of God become visible in Jesus. How is that love made visible through Jesus? It is made visible in the descending way. That is the great mystery of the Incarnation. God has descended to us human beings to become a human being with us; and once among us, descended to the total dereliction of one condemned to death. It isn't easy really to feel and understand from the inside this descending way of Jesus. Every fibre of our being rebels against it. We don't mind paying attention to poor people from time to time; but descending to a state of poverty and becoming poor with the poor, that we don't want to do. And yet that is the way Jesus chose as the way to know God.

In the first century of Christianity there was already a hymn being sung about this descending way of Jesus. Paul puts it into his Letter to the Philippians in order to commend to his people the descending direction on the ladder of life. He writes:

Make your own the mind of Christ Jesus:
Who, being in the form of God,
did not count equality with God
something to be grasped.
But he emptied himself,
taking the form of a slave,
becoming as human beings are;
and being in every way like a human being,
he was humbler yet,
even to accepting death, death on a cross.

Here, expressed in summary but very plain terms, is

36

the way of God's love. It is a way that goes down further and further into the greatest destitution: the destitution of a criminal whose life is taken from him. You may wonder, at this point, whether Jesus isn't a masochist in search of misery. The opposite is true. The gospel of Jesus is a gospel of peace and joy, not of self-disdain and self-torment. The descending way of Jesus is the way to a new fellowship in which we human beings can reach new life and celebrate it happily together.

How is it possible for the descending way of Jesus to give rise to a new kind of community, grounded in love? It's very important that you come to understand this from the inside, so that a desire to follow Jesus in his descending way can gradually grow in you.

As you know, I come to the Netherlands only occasionally and so changes strike me more forcibly than if I were living there all the time. I have noticed one thing in particular: increasing prosperity has not made people more friendly toward one another. They're better off; but that new-found wealth has not resulted in a new sense of community. I get the impression that people are more preoccupied with themselves and have less time for one another than when they didn't possess so much. There's more competitiveness, more envy, more unrest and more anxiety. There's less opportunity to relax, to get together informally, and enjoy the little things in life. Success has isolated a lot of people and made them lonely. It seems sometimes as though meetings between people generally happen on the way to something or someone else.

There's always something else more important, more pressing, of more consequence. The ordinary, simple, little, homely things have to make way for something you really ought to be doing: that film you really should see, that country you simply must visit, and this or that event which you've got to attend. And the higher up you get on the ladder of prosperity, the harder it becomes to be together, to sing together, to pray together and to celebrate life together in a spirit of thanksgiving.

Is it so astonishing, then, that in the Netherlands as in other prosperous countries there are so many people who are lonely, depressed and anxious, and are never genuinely happy? At times, I get the feeling that, under the blanket of success, a lot of people fall asleep in tears. And the question that perhaps lies hidden most deeply in many hearts is the question of love. 'Who really cares about me? Not about my money, my contacts, my reputation or my popularity, but just me? Where do I really feel at home, secure, and cherished? Where can I freely say and think what I like without the fear of losing out on love? Where am I really safe? Where are the people with whom I can simply be, without having to worry about the impression I make on them?'

When I was visiting Bolivia and Peru, I got to know a fair number of poor people. For two months I lived with Pablo and Sofia and their children, Pablito, Maria, and Johnny. Their house was dark and damp, their food inadequate, good clothes too expensive, a good school too far away, and good work, generally speaking, not to be found. And yet . . . it was there that I learned what joy and thankfulness are. It was in that house that I learned to laugh, even to laugh fit to burst. There I learned how to be sociable and to have a really good time, and in that little house I learned something new about love.

When I returned from that visit to rejoin my students in North America and sensed once again their anxiety about the future, the extent of their inner desperation and suicidal melancholy, I had to ask myself once more why it is that God shows his love for us in the descending way of Jesus. The more I thought about it, the more I realized what Jesus was getting at when he said: 'Many who are first will be last, and the last, first.' I was even worried lest my success with the career-makers should in the end deprive me of the love and affection I most longed for. For that reason I decided to seek another way and that's why I've ended up here in Trosly, in the hope of staying closer to the love that lies concealed in poverty.

In the gospel, it's quite obvious that Jesus chose the descending way. He chose it not once but over and over again. At each critical moment he deliberately sought the way downwards. Even though, at twelve years of age, he was already listening to the teachers in the Temple and questioning them, he stayed up to his thirtieth year with his parents in the little-respected town of Nazareth, and was submissive to them. Even though Jesus was without sin, he began his public life by joining the ranks of sinners who were being baptized by John in the Jordan. Even though he was full of divine power, he believed that changing stones into bread, seeking popularity and being counted among the great ones of the earth were temptations.

Again and again you see how Jesus opts for what is small, hidden and poor, and accordingly declines to wield influence. His many miracles always serve to express his profound compassion with suffering humanity; never are they attempts to call attention to himself. As a rule, he even forbids those he has cured to talk to others about it. And as Jesus' life continues to unfold, he becomes increasingly aware that he has been called to fulfil his vocation in suffering and death. In all of this, it becomes plain to us that God has willed to show his love for the world by descending more and more deeply into human frailty. In the four accounts of Jesus' life and death you can see very clearly that the more conscious he becomes of the mission entrusted to him by the Father, the more his realizes that that mission will make him poorer and poorer. He has been sent not only to console poor people, but also to give this consolation as one of them himself. Becoming poor doesn't just mean forsaking house and family, having nowhere to lay one's head, and being increasingly persecuted; it also means parting company with friends, with success, and even with the awareness of God's presence. When, finally, Jesus is hanging on the cross and cries out with a loud voice, 'My God, my God, why have you forsaken me?', only then do we know how far God has gone to show us his love. For it is then that Jesus not only reached his utmost poverty but also showed God's utmost love.

Here we're confronted with a mystery which we can apprehend only in silent prayer. If you try to analyse it, you fall into absurdities that can only sound ridiculous. Who is going to condemn himself to torture and death if he can prevent it? At the moment of his arrest, Jesus said: 'Do you think that I cannot appeal to my Father, who would promptly send more than twelve legions of angels to my defence?' But he does no such thing, for God's way of making love visible is not our way.

God's way can only be grasped in prayer. The more you listen to God speaking within you, the sooner you will hear that voice inviting you to follow the way of Jesus. For Jesus' way is God's way and God's way is not for Jesus only but for everyone who is truly seeking God. Here we come up against the hard truth that the descending way of Jesus is also the way for us to find God. Jesus doesn't hesitate for a moment to make that clear. Soon after he has ended his period of fasting in the wilderness and called his first disciples to follow him, he says:

How blessed are the poor in spirit . . .
Blessed are the gentle . . .
Blessed are those who mourn . . .
Blessed are those who hunger and thirst for uprightness
. . .

40

Blessed are the merciful . . .
Blessed are the pure in heart . . .
Blessed are the peacemakers . . .
Blessed are those who are persecuted in the cause of
uprightness . . .

Jesus is drawing a self-portrait here and inviting his
disciples to become like him. He will continue to speak in
this way to the very end. Jesus never makes a distinction
between himself and his followers. His sorrow will be
theirs; his joy they too will taste. He says: 'If they
persecuted me, they will persecute you too; if they kept
my word, they will keep yours as well.' As he speaks,
they too must speak; as he behaves, they too must behave;
as he suffers, they too must suffer. In all things, Jesus is
their example and even more than that. He is their model.
In his last great prayer to his Father, Jesus prays for his
disciples: 'They do not belong to the world, any more
than I belong to the world . . . As you have sent me into
the world, I have sent them into the world.'

In the final event, Jesus shows that it is love that moves
him to send the disciples as the Father has sent him. Jesus
loves his disciples with the same love that the Father loves
him, and as this love makes Jesus one with the Father,
so too does it make the disciples one with Jesus. Thus, it
is indeed Jesus, himself, who continues his work in his
disciples. Just as that love is made visible in the
descending way of Jesus, so too will it become visible in
our descending way.

As I write this, I'm conscious of how hard it is to express
the richness of the gospel. I would really like to write
about every saying of Jesus because again and again, each
time in a different way, he presents to us the great
mystery of the descending way. It is the way of suffering,
but also the way to healing. It is the way of humiliation,
but also the way to the resurrection. It is the way of tears,

but of tears that turn into tears of joy. It is the way of hiddenness, but also the way that leads to the light that will shine for all people. It is the way of persecution, oppression, martyrdom and death, but also the way to the full disclosure of God's love. In the Gospel of John, Jesus says: 'As Moses lifted up the snake in the desert, so must the Son of man be lifted up.' You see in these words how the descending way of Jesus becomes the ascending way. The 'lifting up' that Jesus speaks of refers both to his being raised up on the cross in total humiliation and to his being raised up from the dead in total glorification.

The descending way of love, the way to the poor, the broken and the oppressed becomes the ascending way of love, the way to joy, peace, and new life. The cross is transformed from a sign of defeat into a sign of victory, from a sign of despair into a sign of hope, from a sign of death into a sign of life.

Every time I see a crucifix, I think about this mystery. Imagine someone setting up a gallows in his living-room and getting a feeling of joy from it. You would judge such a person to be sick. Yet, for us, the cross, a means of execution, has become a sign of liberation. God himself has made the descending way the way to glory. Only when you are prepared to experience this in your own life of prayer and service will you get an inkling of the mystery of God's love.

You are probably wondering how, in imitation of Jesus, you are to find that descending way. That's a very personal and intimate question, and in the end I don't think that anyone can answer it but you. It's not simply a matter of renouncing your money, your possessions, your intellectual formation, or your friends or family. For some people, it has indeed meant this but only because they felt personally called to take that road. Each one of us has to seek out his or her own descending way of love.

That calls for much prayer, much patience and much guidance. It has nothing at all to do with spiritual heroics, dramatically throwing everything overboard to 'follow' Jesus. The descending way is a way that is concealed in each person's heart. But because it is so seldom walked on, it's often overgrown with weeds. Slowly but surely we have to clear the weeds, open the way, and set out on it unafraid.

For me, this weeding out process is always related to prayer, because to pray is to make free time for God, even when you're very busy with important matters of one kind or another. Every time you make free time for God, you clear up a bit of the descending path, and you see where you can plant your feet on the way of love. Nothing spectacular or sensational. It may be simply a matter of what you say, what you read, to whom you speak, where your go on a free afternoon or how you regard yourself and other people. What's fascinating is that the first step invariably makes the second one easier. You begin to discover that love begets love, and step by step you move further forward on the way to God. Gradually, you shed your misgivings about the way of love; you see that 'in love there is no room for fear', and you feel yourself drawn to descend deeper and deeper on the way that Jesus walked before you.

This leads me back to the Eucharist. I have written about the Eucharist in my previous letters; and I want to do the same here because the Eucharist is the sacrament of love, given to us as the means of finding that descending way of Jesus in our hearts. Jesus himself says: 'I am the living bread which has come down from heaven. Anyone who eats this bread will live for ever.' You see here how the descending way of Jesus can become your way too. Whenever you eat the bread of heaven, you not only become more profoundly united with Jesus but you also learn gradually to walk his descending way with him.

Jesus wants to give himself to us so much that he has become food for us and, whenever we eat this food, the longing is aroused also in us to give ourselves away to others. The self-surrendering love which we encounter in the Eucharist is the love that is the source of true Christian community. Paul makes that very clear when he presents the descending way of Jesus to us as the model for living in community. He says: '. . . make my joy complete by being of a single mind, one in love, one in heart and one in mind. Nothing is to be done out of jealousy or vanity; instead, out of humility of mind everyone should give preference to others, everyone pursuing not selfish interests but those of others.'

This mind-set gives concrete form to the descending way of Jesus, who 'did not count equality with God something to be grasped. But he emptied himself, taking the form of a slave'. This is the eucharistic mind. Whenever we eat the body of Jesus and drink his blood, we participate in his descending way in which competitiveness and rivalry have made way for the love of God.

If you yourself are seriously searching for the specific way which you must walk to follow Jesus, then I beg you not to do so on your own but within a eucharistic community. I feel more and more certain that the way of Jesus can't be found outside the community of those who believe in Jesus and make their belief visible by coming together around the eucharistic table. The Eucharist is the heart and centre of being-the-Church. Without it there is no people of God, no community of faith, no Church. Often enough, you see that people who abandon the Church have trouble in holding on to Jesus. This becomes understandable when you consider that the Church is the eucharistic community in which Jesus gives us his body and blood as gifts that come to us from heaven and help us to find the way of love in our own lives.

It's about time to bring this letter to an end. I hope that I've been able to bring Jesus a little closer to you. Here in Trosly we talk about Jesus a lot. Every evening the community of handicapped people and their helpers come together to celebrate the Eucharist. Then Père Thomas preaches a lengthy sermon which is not always easy to follow. Invariably, everyone listens with great attention, even those who, because of their mental handicap, don't understand a thing. Yet these poor people feel themselves very much involved. Full of affection and deeply trusting, they watch this elderly spirit-filled priest. It's as though they understand very well what he's saying, even though it's hard for them to follow his thinking. And then when they all come to receive the body and blood of Jesus, their eyes are filled with joy. They feel privileged to belong to the people of God and don't hesitate to show their gratitude.

I'd be delighted if, in the coming months, you could come and spend a few days here. I'd love to introduce you to the friends I've made and give you a taste of the day-to-day life of the handicapped people and their assistants. It might, perhaps, be the best way to get you to feel something of God's love. Anyway, think about it.

Lots of love to everybody at home.

Until next time,

Henri

LETTER 5

Jesus: the Loving God

Wednesday, 2nd April 1986

My dear Marc,

When I started writing to you, Lent had just begun. I thought then that I'd be able to send you one letter a week. But I seem to have so much to do here in Trosly that I've not been able to live up to my good intentions. It took me five weeks in all to write my letter about the descending way of Jesus. In the meantime, Easter has come round again. It makes me realize how much I am influenced by the liturgical seasons!

During Lent I was so full of the descending way of Jesus which led him to his death, that it would have been hard for me to write about anything else. But now that the daily Bible readings speak of Jesus' victory over death, I notice that I too am thinking differently about Jesus and want to speak of him to you in another way as well. I now see Jesus more in his state of glory and my thoughts are more concerned with the joy of being his disciple. Each part of the liturgical year makes us see Jesus in a different way.

What happened in the Philippines last month alerted me in a new way to the fact that Jesus has come to conquer death. When I was writing my second letter to you, the papers were full of the elections in the Philippines; and I was convinced at the time that the massive electoral fraud designed to keep President Marcos in power would lead to a bloody civil war. Now, a few weeks later, Cory Aquino is president and she has come to power without any resort to violence. For me, this is a hope-filled event, a clear sign that a non-violent victory over a dictatorship is possible.

From various friends who've been following recent events in the Philippines at close quarters, I've heard that we really can speak of a spiritual victory. What happened there involved much more than a political strategy which chanced to be successful. For years past, Christian people, bishops, priests and leading figures in the political life of the country have been familiarizing themselves with the practice of non-violence. Members of the 'Fellowship of Reconciliation' have been organizing retreats aimed at teaching people how to rely on the power of love and, with that power, to defeat the dictatorship. The words of Jesus that go right to the heart of non-violence are well known. Let me write them down for you:

> Love your enemies, do good to those who hate you, bless those who curse you, pray for those who treat you badly. To anyone who slaps you on one cheek, present the other cheek as well; to anyone who takes your cloak from you, do not refuse your tunic. Give to everyone who asks you, and do not ask for your property back from someone who takes it. Treat others as you would like people to treat you . . . love your enemies and do good to them, and lend without any hope of return.

These sayings express not only the essence of non-violent resistance, but also the heart of Jesus' preaching. If anyone should ask you what are the most radical words in the gospel, you need not hesitate to reply: 'Love your enemies.' It's these words that reveal to us most clearly the kind of love proclaimed by Jesus. In these words we have the clearest expression of what it means to be a disciple of Jesus. Love for one's enemy is the touchstone of being a Christian.

Cory Aquino's struggle against the dictatorship in her country was rooted in love for one's enemy. Before she presented herself as a candidate for the presidency, she prayed the whole night for her opponent, Ferdinand Marcos. She knew that hatred would lead to violence. The Filipino bishops and priests supported her and summoned the whole nation to non-violent resistance. When Marcos ordered out his tanks to crush his opponents, the soldiers refused to drive over the people who were praying. Priests wearing alb and stole approached the soldiers, embraced them, and invited them to drop their weapons and pray with the people for reconciliation and peace.

Now that Cory Aquino is herself president, the issue is whether she will be in a position to make love for one's enemy the basis of her government. There are many forces that will make this extremely difficult for her. But whatever happens, we've seen something in the Philippines which a lot of people believed impossible: a resistance to the enemy which was full of love and through which a bloody civil war was prevented.

I've dwelt on the Philippine situation in some detail because it helps me to write concretely about love for one's enemy. As you know, my hope is that through these letters you will get to know Jesus better. I've already described him as the one sent by God, who has descended to us to make God's love visible to us. In this letter I want to say something about the nature of that divine and human love. We human beings use the word 'love' in so many ways that it's hard to talk about God's love without creating confusion. Still, the command of Jesus to love our enemies is, I think, a good starting point for entering more deeply into the mystery of God's love.

The most important thing you can say about God's love is that God loves us not because of anything we've done to earn that love, but because God, in total freedom, has decided to love us. At first sight, this doesn't seem to be very inspiring, but if you reflect on it more deeply this thought can affect and influence your life greatly. We're inclined to see our whole existence in terms of *quid pro quo*; you scratch my back, and I'll scratch yours. We begin by assuming that people will be nice to us if we are nice to them; that they will help us if we help them; that they will invite us if we invite them; that they will love us if we love them. And so the conviction is deeply rooted in us that being loved is something you have to earn. In our pragmatic and utilitarian times this conviction has become even stronger. We can scarcely conceive of getting something for nothing. Everything has to be worked for, even a kind word, an expression of gratitude, a sign of affection.

I think it's this mentality that lies behind a lot of anxiety, unrest, and agitation. It's as though we're forever on the go, trying to prove to each other that we deserve to be loved. The doubt we harbour within us drives us on to ever greater activity. In that way we try to keep our heads above water and not drown in our ever increasing lack of self-respect. The enormous propensity to seek recognition, admiration, popularity, and renown is rooted in the fear that, without all this, we are worthless. You could call it the 'commercialization' of love. Nothing for nothing. Not even love.

The result is a state of mind that makes us live as though our worth as human beings depended on the way others react to us. We allow other people to determine who we are. We think we're good if other people find us to be so; we think we're intelligent if others consider us intelligent; we think we're religious if others think so too.

On the other side, if we're despised, we think at once that we must be contemptible; if we're laughed at, we immediately think we must be ridiculous; if we're ignored, we jump to the conclusion that we're not worth being noticed. And so we submit the most intimate awareness of who we are to the fickle opinions of those around us. Thus, we sell our souls to the world. We're no longer master in our own house. Our friends and enemies decide who we are. We've become the playthings of their good or bad opinions.

In this matter of love we can go further and say that something else, something quite different even, is amiss. Love has not only come to be an emotional bargaining counter, it has also become violent. One can speak nowadays of violent love. I'll unwrap that a little, to show how revealing are Jesus' words: 'Love your enemies.' The more constricted our self-confidence, the greater our need to be reassured. A low opinion of ourselves reinforces our desire to receive signs and tokens of love. In a world in which so many people feel lonely, isolated, and deserted, the longing for love can often take on 'inhuman' proportions. People come to expect more of each other than it's possible to give. When loneliness and low self-esteem become the main source of the longing to be loved, that longing can easily lead to violence. Then, it's as though one person says to another: 'Love me so that I won't feel lonely any more. Love me so that I can believe in myself again at least a little bit.'

The tragic thing, though, is that we humans aren't capable of dispelling one another's loneliness and lack of self-respect. We humans haven't the capacity to relieve one another's most radical predicament. Our ability to satisfy one another's deepest longing is so limited that time and time again we are in danger of disappointing one another. Despite all this, there are times when our longing can be so intense that it blinds us to our mutual limitations and we are tricked into extorting love, even when reason tells us that we can't give one another any total, unlimited, unconditional love. It's then that love becomes violent. It's then that kisses turn into bites, caresses to blows, forgiving looks to suspicious glances, lending a sympathetic ear to eavesdropping, and heartfelt surrender to violation. The borderline between love and violence is frequently transgressed and in our anxiety-ridden times it doesn't take very much to let our desire for love lead us to violent behaviour.

When I look about me and see the many forms of violence present in human relationships, I often have a sense of seeing here, there and everywhere people who want nothing more, nor less, than to be loved, but who have been unable to find any way to express that longing other than through violence, either to others or to themselves. I sometimes get the impression that our prisons are crammed full of people who couldn't express their need to be loved except by flaying about them furiously and hurting other people. At the same time, many of our psychiatric institutions are filled with people who, full of shame and guilt, have given a form to the same need by inflicting damage on themselves. Whether we do violence to others or to ourselves, what we long for in our heart is a non-violent, peaceful communion in which we know ourselves to be secure and loved. But how and where are we to find that non-violent love?

In what I've been describing as violent love, you will, I hope, have detected something of yourself or of the people around you. If so, you will the more readily understand what Jesus means when he speaks of love. Jesus is the revelation of God's unending, unconditional love for us human beings. Everything that Jesus has done, said and undergone is meant to show us that the love we most long for is given to us by God, not because we've deserved it, but because God is a God of love.

51

Jesus has come among us to make that divine love visible and to offer it to us. In his conversation with Nicodemus he says: '. . . this is how God loved the world: he gave his only Son . . . God sent his Son into the world not to judge the world, but so that through him the world might be saved.' In these words the meaning of the Incarnation is summed up. God has become human – that is, God-with-us – in order to show us that the anxious concern for recognition and the violence among us spring from a lack of faith in the love of God. If we had a firm faith in God's unconditional love for us, it would no longer be necessary to be always on the lookout for ways of being admired by people, and we would need, even less, to obtain from people by force what God desires to give us so abundantly.

The descending way of Jesus, painful as it is, is God's most radical attempt to convince us that everything we long for is indeed given us. What he asks of us is to have faith in that love. The word 'faith' is often understood as accepting something you can't understand. People often say: 'Such and such can't be explained, you simply have to believe it.' However, when Jesus talks about faith, he means first of all to trust unreservedly that you are loved, so that you can abandon every false way of obtaining love. That's why Jesus tells Nicodemus that, through faith in the descending love of God, we will be set free from anxiety and violence and will find eternal life. It's a question here of trusting in God's love. The Greek word for faith is *pistis*, which means literally, 'trust'. Whenever Jesus says to the people he has healed: 'Your faith has saved you,' he is saying that they have found new life because they have surrendered in complete trust to the love of God revealed in him.

Trusting in the unconditional love of God: that is the way to which Jesus calls us. The more firmly you grasp this, the more readily will you be able to perceive why

there is so much suspicion, jealousy, bitterness, vindictiveness, hatred, violence and discord in our world. Jesus
himself interprets this by comparing God's love to the
light. He says:

. . . though the light has come into the world
people have preferred
darkness to light
because their deeds were evil.
And indeed, everybody who does wrong
hates the light and avoids it,
to prevent his actions from being shown up;
but whoever does the truth
comes out into the light,
so that what he is doing may plainly appear as done in
   God.

Jesus sees the evil in this world as a lack of trust in God's
love. He makes us see that we persistently fall back on
ourselves, rely more on ourselves than on God, and are
inclined more to love of self than to love of God. So we
remain in the darkness. If we walk in the light, then
we are enabled to acknowledge in joy and gratitude that
everything good, beautiful and true comes from God and
is offered to us in love.

If you come to see this, you'll also understand why
Jesus' words, 'love your enemies,' are among the most
important in the gospel. These words bring us to the heart
and centre of love. As long as love is a matter of 'tit for
tat', we can't love our enemies. Our enemies are those
who withhold love from us and make life difficult for us.
We are inclined spontaneously to hate them and to love
only those who love us.

Jesus, however, will have no part in such bartering. He
says:

If you love those who love you, what credit can you

expect? Even sinners love those who love them. And if you do good to those who do good to you, what credit can you expect? For even sinners do that much. And if you lend to those from whom you hope to get money back, what credit can you expect? Even sinners lend to sinners to get back the same amount.

Jesus shows us that true love, the love that comes from God, makes no distinction between friends and foes, between people who are for us and people who are against us, people who do us a favour and people who do us ill. God makes no such distinction. He loves all human beings, good or bad, with the same unconditional love. This all-embracing love Jesus offers to us, and he invites us to make this love visible in our lives.

If our love, like God's love, embraces foe as well as friend, we have become children of God and are no longer children of suspicion, jealousy, violence, war and death. Our love for our enemies shows to whom we really belong. It shows our true home. Jesus states it so clearly: ' . . . love your enemies and do good to them, and lend without any hope of return. You will have a great reward, and you will be children of the Most High, for he himself is kind to the ungrateful and the wicked.'

There you have it: the love of God is an unconditional love, and only that love can empower us to live together without violence. When we know that God loves us deeply and will always go on loving us, whoever we are and whatever we do, it becomes possible to expect no more of our fellow men and women than they are able to give, to forgive them generously when they have offended us, and always to respond to their hostility with love. By doing so we make visible a new way of being human and a new way of responding to our world problems.

Mrs Aquino realized that hatred for President Marcos

could not lead to peace in the Philippines: Martin Luther King understood that hating whites could not lead to true equality among Americans. Gandhi knew that hating the British could not bring about genuine independence in India. A new world without slaughter and massacre can never be the fruit of hatred. It is the fruit of the love of 'your Father in heaven, for he causes his sun to rise on the bad as well as the good, and sends down rain to fall on the upright and the wicked alike.' It is the fruit of God's love which we limited humans are to make visible in our lives in accordance with the words of Jesus: 'You must therefore set no bounds to your love, just as your heavenly Father sets none to his.'

Whenever, contrary to the world's vindictiveness, we love our enemy, we exhibit something of the perfect love of God, whose will is to bring all human beings together as children of one Father. Whenever we forgive instead of letting fly at one another, bless instead of cursing one another, tend one another's wounds instead of rubbing salt into them, hearten instead of discouraging one another, give hope instead of driving one another to despair, hug instead of harassing one another, welcome instead of cold-shouldering one another, thank instead of criticizing one another, praise instead of maligning one another . . . in short, whenever we opt for and not against one another, we make God's unconditional love visible; we are diminishing violence and giving birth to a new community.

I hope you feel that we are touching here the heart of the gospel. Jesus challenges us to move in a totally new direction. He asks for conversion, that is to say, a complete interior turn-around, a transformation. Not an easy thing, as is certainly evident from his words: 'But it is a narrow gate and a hard road that leads to life, and only a few find it.' Everything within us seems set against this way. And yet . . . every time we take a few steps along it, we become aware that something new is happening within us and experience a desire to try yet another step forward. And so, step by step, we come closer to the heart of God, which is the heart of an undiscriminating, always-forgiving, inexhaustible love. This might look like a very tall order, especially when you're facing it alone. You've often told me about your classmates' cynical reactions whenever you talk about Jesus. It is, indeed, very difficult to look for the way to the heart of God without the support of your friends. That's why it's important to ask yourself with whom you intend to look. You need a community, even if it's a fairly small one. For myself, I've enjoyed a lot of support from one or two friends with whom I was able to share my spiritual adventure. It's practically impossible to lay yourself open to other people who are ill disposed or indifferent toward you. Real vulnerability can only be fruitful in a community of people who are searching for God together. So one of your most important tasks is to find friends who want to walk with you on the long road of conversion.

Still, there are a number of concrete steps which you yourself can take here and now in order to arrive at this conversion.

In this letter I want to limit myself to a few thoughts about prayer and the Eucharist. If you wish to learn the love of God, you have to begin by praying for your enemies. That's not as easy as it may sound. Praying for people requires wanting the best for them, and that's far from easy if it has to do with a fellow student who speaks ill of you, a girl who finds someone else more attractive than you, a 'friend' who gets you to do all those awkward little chores for him, or a colleague who's trying his best to get your job. But each time you pray, really pray, for your enemies, you'll notice that your heart is being made new. Within your prayer, you quickly discover that your enemies are in fact your fellow human beings loved by

God just as much as yourself. The result is that the walls you've thrown up between 'him and me', 'us and them', 'ours and theirs' disappear. You heart grows deeper and broader and opens up more and more to all the human beings with whom God in his love has peopled the earth.

I find it difficult to conceive of a more concrete way to love than by praying for one's enemies. It makes you conscious of the hard fact that, in God's eyes, you're no more and no less worthy of being loved than any other person, and it creates an awareness of profound solidarity with all other human beings. It creates in you a world-embracing compassion and provides you in increasing measure with a heart free of the compulsive urge to coercion and violence. And you'll be delighted to discover that you can no longer remain angry with people for whom you've really and truly prayed. You will find that you start speaking differently to them or about them, and that you are actually willing to do good to those who've offended you in some way.

To end, I want to return to the subject of the Eucharist. In the Eucharist God's love is most concretely made present. Jesus has not only become human, he has also become bread and wine in order that, through our eating and our drinking, God's love might become our own. The great mystery of the Eucharist is that God's love is offered to us not in the abstract, but in a very concrete way; not as a theory, but as food for our daily life. The Eucharist opens the way for us to make God's love our own. Jesus himself makes that clear to us when he says:

. . . my flesh is real food
and my blood is real drink.
Whoever eats my flesh and drinks my blood
lives in me
and I live in that person.

As the living Father sent me
and I draw life from the Father,
so whoever eats me will also draw life from me.

Whenever you receive the body and blood of Jesus in
the Eucharist, his love is given to you, the same love that
he showed on the cross. It is the love of God for all people
of all times and places, all religions and creeds, all races
and classes, all tribes and nations, all sinners and saints.
On the cross, Jesus has shown us how far God's love
goes. It's a love which embraces even those who crucified
him. When Jesus is hanging nailed to the cross, totally
broken and stripped of everything, he still prays for his
executioners: 'Father, forgive them; they do not know
what they are doing.' Jesus's love for his enemies knows
no bounds. He prays even for those who are putting him
to death. It is this, the enemy-loving love of God, that is
offered to us in the Eucharist. To forgive our enemies
doesn't lie within our power. That is a divine gift. That's
why it's so important to make the Eucharist the heart and
centre of your life. It's there that you receive the love
which empowers you to take the way that Jesus has taken
before you: a narrow way, a painful way, but the way
that gives you true joy and peace and enables you to
make the non-violent love of God visible in this world.
I began this letter by discussing events in the Philippines. The non-violent resistance to President Marcos's
dictatorship made a big impression on me and prompted
me to write to you about love for one's enemy as the core
of Jesus' preaching. That the events in the Philippines
were exceptional is evident from the fact that, as I
conclude this letter, the papers are full of the American
attack on Libya. Colonel Gaddaffi's terrorism has resulted
in the use of force by the United States. Violence on the
one side has provoked it on the other. Now everyone is
afraid that the violence may spread like an oil slick on the

water. It's the endless chain of hatred and retaliation. Despite the fact that those who wield power in our world persist in thinking that they can counter force with force, the opposite proves to be the case over and over again. Violence invariably breeds violence. Mrs Aquino's example of non-violent resistance is not emulated. It's still an exception but, nevertheless, a sign of hope.

I earnestly pray that you will cling to those small signs of hope and not let yourself be led astray by the noise and clamour of those who persist in relying on violence. The way of Jesus is not self-evident but it is the only way that leads to life and can save our world from total destruction. Let us hope and pray with all our hearts that we may have the courage and the confidence to follow the way of Jesus to the end.

My warmest greetings to your father and mother, and to Frédérique and Reinier.

With much affection, till next time,

Henri

LETTER 6

Jesus: the Hidden God

Friday, 18th April 1986

My dear Marc,

This letter comes to you from Châteauneuf de Galaure, a small village in the Drome region, south of Lyons and east of the Rhône. I'm surprised at myself for being here. Before I went to France I'd never heard of Châteauneuf de Galaure, and now, eight months on, it's become for me one of the most important places in the world. That probably sounds exaggerated to you, but I hope you'll understand by the time you've finished reading this letter.

During my first month in Trosly I kept hearing the name of someone entirely unknown to me: Marthe Robin. Often, when someone tried to tell me how he or she had come to have a deep faith in Jesus, I would hear: 'It was Marthe who set me on the right path.' I discovered, too, that her name was associated with a number of new spiritual movements in France. Wherever I tried to get a better insight into the development of French spirituality, I heard the name of Marthe Robin.

As you can imagine, I became increasingly curious. I began reading books about her and asking for more and more information. Then one day Thérèse Monique, a friend of mine in Trosly, said to me: 'Marthe Robin was born, lived, and died in Châteauneuf de Galaure. If you want to discover the deeper significance of her life, you should go and spend the inside of a week there. Two good friends of mine, Bernard and Claudine, live very near Châteauneuf and they'll be glad to put you up. I will be glad to take you there in the car.' She was as good as her word.

It's now April 18th, a Friday, I've been with Bernard and Claudine since last Sunday, and throughout the week I've had time and opportunity to find out about Marthe Robin's life and to understand why she's had and still has such an influence on the spiritual life inside France and, to an increasing extent, outside France as well.

I'd like to tell you one or two things about her, not just because I happen to be here but because, all along, I've been wanting to write to you about Jesus as the hidden God. I don't think you'll ever be able to penetrate the mystery of God's revelation in Jesus until it strikes you that the major part of Jesus' life was hidden and that even the 'public' years remained invisible as far as most people were concerned. Whereas the way of the world is to insist on publicity, celebrity, popularity and getting maximum exposure, God prefers to work in secret. You must let that mystery of God's secrecy, God's anonymity, sink deeply into your consciousness because, otherwise, you're continually looking at it from the wrong point of view. In God's sight, the things that really matter seldom take place in public. It's quite possible that the reasons why God sustains our violent and homicidal world and continues giving us new opportunities for conversion will always remain unknown to us. Maybe, while we focus our whole attention on the VIPs and their movements, on peace conferences and protest demonstrations, it's the totally unknown people, praying and working in silence, who make God save us yet again from destruction. I often think that I've succeeded in staying true to my Christian and priestly calling thanks to the prayers and magnanimity of people who remain completely unknown to me during my lifetime. Maybe the greatest saints remain anonymous!

Marthe Robin is one of the most impressive examples of God's hidden presence in our world. She was born in 1902. At sixteen years she fell ill, and her illness, for which the doctors could find no explanation, grew worse and worse. Slowly but surely she became aware that God was calling her to a life in which she would be linked in a special way to the suffering of Jesus. When she was twenty-three, she wrote an 'act of abandonment'. In it she gave to the God of love all that she had: her memory, her reason and her will; her body with all its senses, her mind with all its faculties, her heart with all its feelings. She writes: 'I belong to you without any reservations, forever. O Beloved of my soul! It is you only whom I want, and for your love I renounce all.'*

When she was twenty-six, her legs became totally paralyzed and soon afterwards her arms. From then on she did not eat, drink or sleep. From 1928 until her death in 1981, she took no food other than weekly Holy Communion. When I first heard about this, it sounded to me like a pious fairy tale, but now that I've talked to a lot of people who knew Marthe Robin personally, I realize that God can achieve a great deal more in a human being than we, people of little faith, are prepared to believe possible. The total 'abstinence' of Marthe is one of the ways in which Jesus showed his love to her.

In September 1930 Jesus appeared to Marthe and asked her: 'Do you wish to become as I am?' She said: 'Yes,' and soon afterwards she received the wounds of Jesus in her hands, feet and side. She also received the crown of thorns. From that time on, week by week, Marthe began

* Raymond Peyret, *Marthe Robin*, (New York, Alba House, 1983), p. 39.

to enter fully into the Passion of Jesus. Her suffering with Jesus was so intense that tears of blood flowed from her eyes and the marks of invisible thorns appeared across her head.

Every Friday she entered so fully into the death of Jesus that only on Saturday did she come to herself again; and then until Sunday or Monday she remained in a state of total exhaustion. As the years passed, her suffering grew deeper. In the beginning she suffered *with* Jesus, but little by little she *became* the suffering Jesus. To Jean Guitton, a well-known French philosopher who visited her several times, she said:

> At the start, I recognized in my visions people along the road that Jesus took to Calvary. But now I've gone beyond that. What occupies me now is the Passion, uniquely Jesus. I don't know how I am to explain it . . . Things like that are so grievous that you would die if God did not support you. And yet it's exquisite.*

I'm not telling you all this for the sake of relating something uncanny or gloomy or weird, but to show you that, in the midst of our warring world, there are people who, in a very hidden way, enter into the mystery of Jesus' suffering, a suffering for the world's sake. This happened back in the thirteenth century with St Francis of Assisi, and it has happened in our lifetime with Marthe Robin.

A number of times now, I've gone to pray in the room where, for fifty-one years, Marthe experienced the suffering of Jesus. Many of those who knew her say that there has probably never been anyone who has lived out so directly and so fully in their own body the suffering and death of Jesus. Every time I walk into that little room, I experience what I have so far never experienced anywhere else: a peace which the world cannot give, a

---

* Jean Guitton, *Portrait de Marthe Robin*, (Paris, Grasset, 1985), p. 199.

joy which doesn't conflict with suffering, a total surrender which makes true freedom possible, and a love which comes from God himself but which often remains unknown to us human beings. There I discover quite concretely what life is about and what is asked of me if I want to spread the love of God. It's a life in which joy and the cross are never separated. It's a life which doesn't seek influence, power, success and popularity, but trusts that God is secretly at work and, in secret, is causing something new to grow. It's a life of mortification, that is to say, of dying to old ways of being so as to make it possible for us to bear new fruit.

Many people came to visit Marthe during her lifetime to seek her advice and counsel. In utter simplicity and often with a great sense of humour she would chat with them. It was extremely rare for her to talk about herself. Her concern and compassion were always directed towards her guests. Not infrequently, she would understand them even before they had asked her anything. Sometimes she would give quite explicit instructions, sometimes she only asked questions, but always people left her room with a profound feeling of inner peace.

It's no exaggeration to say that the renewal of the French Church began, to a great extent, with Marthe: in God's name she asked her spiritual director to start new Christian schools and to build retreat houses; she stressed the importance of the laity in the Church; she inspired priests to initiate new religious communities, and she helped people decide whether to marry or to enter a religious order. The renewal and deepening of religious life in France is inconceivable without her. After her death on 6th February, 1981, her influence became greater than ever. Jesus says: '. . . unless a wheat grain falls into the earth and dies, it remains only a single grain; but if it dies, it yields a rich harvest.' Only now, after Marthe's death, is the full significance of her life becoming apparent.

Whenever I see the small French homestead where Marthe spent her days and talk with the two old ladies who looked after her year by year and even now still welcome the people who come to pray in her room, I'm reminded of Jesus' words: 'I bless you, Father, Lord of heaven and of earth, for hiding these things from the learned and the clever and revealing them to little children.' While the most frightful things were happening in Europe and while two world wars were unveiling the demonic dimensions of evil, Jesus disclosed to a frail countrywoman in France his unfathomable love for humankind.

You see here an aspect of Jesus which we can easily forget. Jesus is the hidden God. He became a human being among a small, oppressed people, under very difficult circumstances. He was held in contempt by the rulers of his country and was put to a shameful death between two criminals.

There was nothing spectacular about Jesus' life. Far from it! Even when you look at Jesus' miracles, you find that he did not heal or revive people in order to get publicity. He frequently forbade them even to talk about it. His resurrection too was a hidden event. Only his disciples and a few of the women and men who had known him intimately before his death saw him as the risen Lord.

Now that Christianity has become one of the major world religions and millions of people utter the name of Jesus every day, it's hard for us to believe that Jesus revealed God in hiddenness. But neither Jesus' life nor his death nor his resurrection were intended to astound us with the great power of God. God became a lowly, hidden, almost invisible God.

I'm constantly struck by the fact that wherever the

gospel of Jesus bears fruit, we come across this hiddenness. The great Christians throughout history have always
been lowly people who sought to be hidden. Benedict hid
himself in the vale of Subiaco, Francis in the Carceri
outside Assisi, Ignatius in the grotto of Manresa, the little
Thérèse in the Carmel of Lisieux. Whenever you hear
about saintly people, you sense a deep longing for that
hiddenness, that seclusion. We so easily forget it, but Paul
too withdrew into the wilderness for two years before he
started on his preaching mission.

The initial reaction of someone who has a really
personal encounter with Jesus is not to start shouting it
from the rooftops but, rather, to dwell secretly in the
presence of God. It is very important for you to realize
that perhaps the greater part of God's work in this world
may go unnoticed. There are a number of people who in
these days have become widely known as great saints or
influential Christians: Mother Teresa in Calcutta, Bishop
Romero in El Salvador, Padre Pio in Italy and Dorothy
Day in New York; but the greatest part of God's work in
our history could well remain completely unknown.
That's a mystery which is difficult to grasp in an age that
attaches so much value to publicity. We tend to think that
the more people know and talk about something, the
more important it must be. That's understandable,
considering the fact that great notoriety often means big
money, and big money often means a large degree of
power, and power easily creates the illusion of importance. In our society, it's often statistics that determine
what's important: the best-selling LP, the most popular
book, the richest man, the highest tower-block, the most
expensive car. With the enormous growth of advertizing
it's become nearly impossible to believe that what's really
important happens in secret.

Yet . . . we do have some intimations of this. A human
life begins in the seclusion of the womb, and the most

determinative experiences occur in the privacy of the family. The seedling grows in the seclusion of the soil, and the egg is hatched in the seclusion of the nest. Like creativity, intimacy too needs seclusion. We know intuitively that everything which moves us by its delicacy, vulnerability and pristine beauty can stand only very little public exposure. The mass media which magnify creativity and intimacy are proof of that. What is precious and sacred in hiddenness often becomes cheap and even vulgar when exposed to the public at large by the mass media. Publicity standardizes, hardens and, not infrequently, suffocates what it exposes.

Many great minds and spirits have lost their creative force through too early or too rapid exposure to the public. We know it; we sense it; but we easily forget it because our world persists in proclaiming the big lie: 'Being unknown means being unloved.' If you're ready to trust your intuition and so preserve a degree of healthy scepticism in the face of the current propaganda you are more likely to detect the hidden presence of God. It strikes me again and again that, in our publicity-seeking world, a lot of discussions about God take it as their starting point that even God has to justify himself. People often say: 'If that God of yours really exists, then why doesn't he make his omnipotence more visible in this chaotic world of ours?' God is called to account, as it were, and mockingly invited to prove, just for once, that he really does exist. Again, you often hear someone say: 'I've no need whatever for God. I can perfectly well look after myself. As a matter of fact, I've yet to receive any help from God with my problems!' The bitterness and sarcasm evident in remarks of this sort show what's expected: that God should at least be concerned about his own popularity. People often talk as though God has as great a need for recognition as we do.

Now look at Jesus who came to reveal God to us, and

you see that popularity in any form is the very thing he avoids. He is constantly pointing out that God reveals himself in secrecy. It sounds very paradoxical, but accepting and, I would venture to say, entering into that paradox sets you on the road of the spiritual life.

With these thoughts about the hidden revelation of Jesus, is it now possible for you to start moving spiritually? I think you can, because the truth, that Jesus makes himself known to you in secret, requires that you start looking for him in your own seclusion. It is *his* seclusion, *his* hiddenness, that invites you to enter into your own.

And here we're back again with the mystery of our own heart. Our heart is at the centre of our being human. There our deepest thoughts, intuitions, emotions and decisions find their source. But it's also there that we are often most alienated from ourselves. We know little or nothing of our own heart. We keep our distance, as though we were afraid of it. What is most intimate is also what frightens us most. Where we are most ourselves, we are often strangers to ourselves. That is the painful part of our being human. We fail to know our hidden centres; and so we live and die often without knowing who we really are. If we ask ourselves why we think, feel and act in such or such a way, we often have no answer, thus proving to be strangers in our own house.

The mystery of the spiritual life is that Jesus desires to meet us in the seclusion of our own heart, to make his love known to us there, to free us from our fears and to make our own deepest self known to us. In the privacy of our heart, therefore, we can learn not only to know Jesus but, through Jesus, ourselves as well. If you reflect on this a bit more, you will see an interaction between God's love revealing itself to you and a constant growth in your self-knowledge. Each time you let the love of God penetrate deeper into your heart, you lose a bit of your anxiety, and every time you shed a bit of your anxiety, you learn to know yourself better and long all the more to be known by your loving God.

Thus, the more you learn to love God, the more you learn to know and to cherish yourself. Self-knowledge and self-love are the fruit of knowing and loving God. You can see better now what is intended by the great commandment to 'love the Lord your God with all your heart, with all your soul, and with all your mind, and to love your neighbour as yourself'. Laying our hearts totally open to God leads to a love of ourselves that enables us to give whole-hearted love to our fellow human beings. In the seclusion of our hearts we learn to know the hidden presence of God; and with that spiritual knowledge we can lead a loving life.

But all of this requires discipline. The spiritual life demands a discipline of the heart. Discipline is the mark of a disciple of Jesus. This doesn't mean, however, making things difficult for yourself, but making available the inner space where God can touch you with an all-transforming love. We human beings are so faint-hearted that we have a lot of trouble leaving an empty space empty. We like to fill it all up with ideas, plans, duties, tasks, and activities.

It strikes me increasingly just how hard-pressed people are nowadays. It's as though they're tearing about from one emergency to another. Never solitary, never still, never really free but always busy about something that just can't wait. You get the impression that, amid this frantic hurly-burly, we lose touch with life itself. We have the experience of being busy while nothing real seems to happen. The more agitated we are, and the more compacted our lives become, the more difficult it is to keep a space where God can let something truly new take place.

The discipline of the heart helps us to let God into our hearts so that God can become known to us there, in the deepest recesses of our own being. This is not so easy to do; we like to be master in our own house and don't want to admit that our house is God's house too. God wants to be together with us where we really live and, by loving us there, to show us the way to be a complete human being. God's love is a demanding, even a jealous love, and when we let that love speak within us, we are led into places where we would often rather not go.

And yet we know that everyone who has let God's love enter into his or her heart has not only become a better human being, but has also contributed significantly to making a better world. The lives of the saints show us that. And so I say: Make room in your heart for God and let God cherish you. There you can be alone with God. There heart speaks to heart and there in that holy seclusion the new person will be born in you. Jesus said to Nicodemus: '. . . no one can see the kingdom of God without being born from above.' It is this rebirth that is made possible when you dare to be alone with God. It takes place in the deepest secrecy, but its effect reaches to the ends of the earth. Where God's heart speaks to your heart, there everything is made new.

In this letter too I want to come back for a moment to the Eucharist; for the Eucharist is pre-eminently the sacrament of God's hiddenness. What is more ordinary than a piece of bread and a sip of wine? What is simpler than the words: 'Take and eat, take and drink. This is my body and blood . . . Do this as a memorial of me?'

I've often stood with friends around a small table, taken bread and wine and said the words which Jesus spoke when he took leave of his disciples. Nothing pretentious, nothing spectacular, no crowd of people, no stirring songs, no formality. Just a few people eating a piece of bread and drinking a little wine, not enough bread to make a meal and not enough wine to quench a thirst.

And yet, . . . in this hiddenness the risen Jesus is present, and God's love is revealed. Just as God became a human being for us in hiddenness, so too in hiddenness he becomes food and drink for us. What anyone can pass by, unheeding, is actually the greatest event that can happen among us human beings.

In the course of my stay at L'Arche in France I discovered how closely God's hiddenness in the Eucharist is connected with hiddenness in God's people.

I still remember Mother Teresa once saying to me that you can't see God in the poor unless you can see him in the Eucharist. At the time, that remark seemed to me a bit high-flying and pious; but now that I've spent a year living with handicapped people, I'm beginning to understand better what she meant. It isn't really possible to see God in human beings if you can't see him in the hidden reality of the bread that comes down from heaven. In human beings you can see this, that, and the other: angels and devils, saints and brutes, benevolent souls and malevolent power-maniacs. However, it's only when you've learned from personal experience how much Jesus cares for you and how much he desires to be your daily food, that you can learn to see every human heart as a dwelling place for Jesus. When your heart is touched by the presence of Jesus in the Eucharist, then you will receive new eyes capable of recognizing that same presence in the hearts of others. Heart speaks to heart. Jesus in our heart speaks to Jesus in the hearts of our fellow men and women. That's the eucharistic mystery of which we are part.

We want to see results and preferably instantly. But God works in secret and with a divine patience. By taking part in the Eucharist you can come gradually to understand this. Then your heart can begin to open up to the God who suffers in the people around you.

I began this letter by talking about Marthe Robin. For

71

more than fifty years the only food she took was the eucharistic bread, brought to her once a week. Jesus was indeed her whole being. Because of this she could teach her visitors how to discover Jesus in their own hearts. For many of them that discovery was the beginning of a radical spiritual transformation.

When we know through personal experience that God does indeed live in us, we are able, like Jesus himself, to work miracles and to change the face of the earth. Not by seeking publicity, but by constantly seeking Jesus in the hidden centre of our lives and the lives of our fellow men and women.

Dear Marc, I hope that in this letter I've been able to bring you a little closer to Jesus as the hidden God. I shall leave it at this. In my next letter, a final one, I want to offer you some suggestions for living, day by day, a life in which Jesus is, and will always be, at the centre.

Warmest greetings to your mother and father and to Frédérique and Reinier.

Yours affectionately,

Henri

LETTER 7

Listening to Jesus

Thursday, 18th September 1986

My dear Marc,

It was more than seven months ago that I began writing these letters about the spiritual life. I sent you the first three from West Germany and the three later ones from France. That time now seems far away and long ago.

In mid-August I went to Canada to live and work at 'Daybreak', the L'Arche community near Toronto. This morning I read through my letters to you once more, and I realized that I'd probably written them as much for myself as for you. My year in Europe was meant to be a period of searching for a new direction in my life. I had a vague notion that Jesus was calling me to leave the university and to go and live with mentally handicapped people. My meeting with Jean Vanier and my stay in the L'Arche community at Trosly awoke in me something new which I couldn't continue to ignore. The burning question was: 'How best am I to follow Jesus?'

In my letters I've tried to bring you closer to Jesus. But I now realize that I've also 'used' these letters to get to know Jesus better myself and so become better able to hear the invitation to follow him. It's good, I think, that these letters have a purpose for both of us because it's only with what touches my heart that I am able to touch yours.

In my very first letter, I said that I could write to you only what I've lived through and experienced myself. In this final letter I can honestly say that everything I have written to you has sprung directly from my own searching for God. I hope this will prove more of a help than a hindrance for you. My greatest desire was to awaken in you a deep love for Jesus. I've told you of the Jesus who liberates, of the suffering Jesus and his compassion, of the Jesus who in his humility chose the descending way, of the loving Jesus who challenges us to love even our enemies, and finally of the Jesus of Nazareth who reveals to us the mystery of God's hiddenness. As you see, I've begun with the end of the gospel and ended with the beginning. In doing that I've tried to stay close to the Church's proclamation, which approaches the mysteries of God's incarnation and redemption from the perspective of its faith in the risen Lord.

In the course of writing I've discovered for myself the great extent to which I'm inclined to 'secularize' Jesus. Instinctively, I look to Jesus for a cheap liberation, a solution to my problems, help with my desire for success, getting even with my opponents, and a good measure of publicity. It's not always easy to see Jesus as the gospel presents him; as the Lord who calls us to spiritual freedom, shares our suffering, shows us the descending way, challenges us to love our enemies and secretly reveals God's love to us. And yet, each time I catch a glimpse of the real Jesus, I'm conscious of a new inward peace, and it is again possible to recognize his voice and follow it.

So I can tell you that these letters have helped me to see the real Jesus and have strengthened my decision to go to Canada and live and work there with mentally handicapped people.

Spiritual life is life lived in the spirit of Jesus. I've spoken of the Eucharist as being the centre of that life. Jesus is more, much more, than an important historical figure who can still inspire us today. In the Eucharist, he sets us free from constraint and compulsion, unites our suffering with his, forms a fellowship in shared vulner-ability, offers us a love that forgives even our enemies and helps us to see God in the seclusion of the human heart. Where the Eucharist is, there Jesus really is present; there too the Church really is a body, and there we really do share, even now, in eternal life.

You and I, both, are called to be disciples of Jesus. The differences between us in age, circumstances, upbringing, and experience are small matters compared with the calling we have in common. What counts is being attentive at all times to the voice of God's love inviting us to obey, that is, to listen with an attentive heart.

How can we keep listening to this voice in a world which does its best to distract us and get our attention for seemingly more urgent matters? In this last letter I want to put before you, by way of a conclusion, three forms of listening that, for me, have proven to be the most productive.

First of all, listen to the Church. I know that that isn't a popular bit of advice at a time and in a country where the Church is frequently seen more as an 'obstacle' in the way' rather than as the 'the way' to Jesus. Nevertheless, I'm profoundly convinced that the greatest spiritual danger for our times is the separation of Jesus from the Church. The Church is the body of the Lord. Without Jesus there can be no Church; and without the Church we cannot stay united with Jesus. I've yet to meet anyone who has come closer to Jesus by forsaking the Church. To listen to the Church is to listen to the Lord of the Church. Specifically, this means taking part in the Church's liturgical life. Advent, Christmas, Lent, Easter,

Ascension and Pentecost; these seasons and feasts teach you to know Jesus better and better, and unite you more and more intimately with the divine life he offers you in the Church.

The Eucharist is the heart of the Church's life. It's there that you hear the life-giving gospel and receive the gifts that sustain that life within you. The best assurance that you'll keep listening to the Church is your regular participation in the Eucharist.

Secondly, listen to the book. By that I mean read the Bible; read books about the Bible, about the spiritual life and the lives of 'great' saints. I know you read a good deal; but a lot of what you read distracts you from the way that Jesus is showing you. The secondary school and university offer you little in the way of 'spiritual reading'. That's why it's very important for you to read regularly books which will help you in your spiritual life. Many people are brought to God through spiritual literature which they chance or choose to read. Augustine, Ignatius, Thomas Merton, and many others have been converted through the book. The secret, however, is not to use a 'spiritual' book as a source of interesting information, but rather to listen to it as to a voice that addresses you directly. It isn't easy to let a text 'read' you. Your thirst for knowledge and information often makes you desire to own the word, instead of letting the word own you. Even so, you will learn the most by listening carefully to the Word that seeks admission to your heart.

Finally, listen to your heart. It's there that Jesus speaks most intimately to you. Praying is first and foremost listening to Jesus who dwells in the very depths of your heart. He doesn't shout. He doesn't thrust himself upon you. His voice is an unassuming voice, very nearly a whisper, the voice of a gentle love. Whatever you do with your life, go on listening to the voice of Jesus in your heart. This listening must be an active and very attentive listening, for in our restless and noisy world God's so loving voice is easily drowned out. You need to set aside some time every day for this active listening to God if only for ten minutes. Ten minutes each day for Jesus alone can bring about a radical change in your life.

You'll find that it isn't easy to be still for ten minutes at a time. You'll discover straightaway that many other voices, voices that are very noisy and distracting, voices which do not come from God, demand your attention. But if you stick to your daily prayer time, then slowly but surely you'll come to hear the gentle voice of love and will long more and more to listen to it.

These three ways of listening will guide you to an ever-deepening spiritual life. They will help you to get to know Jesus in a very intimate way, make you aware of the unique manner in which he is calling you, and give you the courage to follow him even to places where you'd rather not go. Living with Jesus is a great adventure. It's the adventure of love. When you admit Jesus to your heart, nothing is predictable; but everything becomes possible. I pray that you will venture on a life with Jesus. He asks everything of you, but gives you more in return. With all my heart I wish you much hope, much courage, and abounding confidence.

Affectionate greetings to your parents, and to Frédérique and Reinier.

Yours affectionately,

Henri

Index of Biblical Quotations